The Annelid Poet

The Annelid Poet

Tristram Cole

The Annelid Poet
Copyright © 2012 by Tristram Cole
All rights reserved. Except for brief passages quoted in a newspaper, online, or in some other forum of the media, no part of this publication may be reproduced or transmitted in any form or by any means other than skywriting without express written permission from the author.

First edition, printed by CreateSpace

ISBN-13: 978-1475109504
ISBN-10: 1475109504

For Jennie, who takes care of me

Table of Contents

Preorifice

The Annelid Poet

1998	one
1999	seven
2000	eighteen
2001	thirty-three
2002	forty-two
2003	fifty-seven

After the Worm

2004	seventy-two
2005	eighty-five
2006	ninety-one
2007	one hundred one
2008	one sixteen
2009	one seventeen
2010	one nineteen
2011	one twenty-eight

Worms Don't Have Appendices

Notes

Preorifice

Annelid here, welcoming my fellow worms to a savory repast. Before filling your ample coeloms with the masticated pulp of my fancy however, I must ask that you pause momentarily, to reflect on a rather indigestible matter – one of form.

You see, the poet's task isn't quite what it was. Nor is art so very clean anymore. Pretty things, it turns out, get rather grubby up close, which is fine for most worms of course because they don't care, but not so for the defiant, the fastidious ones. Nope – there's a whole subphylum th't just don't know how to get down and dirty, won't even admit t' life's inherent filthiness. I'm not sayin' that's bad – no – all I'm sayin' is they gotta understand a few things about the rest of us.

Me, I've been trailin' slime for near on forty years, 'n if there's one thing I've learned it's that you can't get anywhere without first startin' to crawl. Sure, you can have the idea of somethin' in your ganglion, but you gotta move toward it to get there. Now, books 've been skippin' how you get there since forever, but not this one – I'm gonna inch my way right from the start. Sure it may seem like I'm just wrigglin' in place at times but believe me, I'm gettin' somewhere, findin' an end. Maybe I'll double back, who knows. Maybe I'll drown in a heavy rain. No matter though: I'll see you on the other side.

The Annelid Poet

1998

  I went out to the end of the dock and looked straight down through the water to where the sunbeams don't reach any farther. I must have needed to scare myself so I did things like that. There is a tree on that beach that kind of stands closer to the water than the rest. Maybe I'd climb that tree and pretend it was going to get torn up by the wind and thrown way out into the middle of the lake. Flying for a few seconds like that would be so unheard of and fantastic and strange. Imagine you're at the beach or on your boat just sitting or maybe trolling and this tree goes flying by with a boy holding onto it – you watch until it goes around a little island or something and then it's gone.

  I never tell people those types of things because they're personal. Once I swear I saw a red light high up in the sky on Christmas Eve slowly moving, getting brighter and brighter, heading right toward my neighborhood, and I knew exactly who it had to be but I didn't tell anyone – it was like only I was supposed to see, like I was *the* person in my family who got to see. I wish I'd woken up my brother and told him now – I mean, I swear I could even barely hear sleigh bells out there. It was right after that Christmas I think when I found out about Santa being a story, but I couldn't get that picture out of my head of me looking up from my bed through the window seeing that light up there with everyone else asleep and how I felt.

My dad and mom woke me and my brother up this one time when we were at camp and made us come down to the beach there and look at the Northern Lights. I was into cowboy boots then I guess because I remember I was wearing shorts and my cowboy boots. My brother was complaining and I didn't care much either but I don't think I complained too. It must have been really late at night – all I can remember is we were all standing on the beach and my brother was squirming around and my parents wouldn't let go of our hands.

Sometimes I'm out walking on the paths behind my house through the woods and I think about how this path could be in another state but it isn't – it's just here and there's just me here to appreciate it so I'll run really fast and duck under tree branches and dodge bushes breathing really hard like someone's chasing me, until I come to where the path turns into an old road or ends behind somebody's house. I'll run like that and I nearly scare myself – it's weird – and then I'll think of this dream I had about a giant bee that runs on two legs and stings people through the back when it catches up to them. So then I'll kind of jog back home so it seems like I don't care and later I'll think about things like walking the paths and seeing faces through the trees when I'm standing in my towel in front of the woodstove. Boy I sure can scare myself sometimes.

There's this swamp near my house down a hill in the woods and I found a tree fort there once and I've never been able to find it since. Swamps are like that because of all the water and quicksand and rotten wood in the way. The puddles there get almost ten feet deep and who knows what lives in them. People are always vanishing in swamps I guess but I love them because there's so much to do – you can measure how deep the little ponds are, you can throw things in, play hide-and-seek around them – and they are dangerous, with poisonous plants and salamanders and dead things.

In my backyard a ways into the woods there is this place where all the trees are dead – my brother and I call it the dead woods – and it's the best place for kindling. It's a nice place to visit but don't stay there too long – it gets kind of sad and creepy, like maybe someone died there or is buried there and they like to give us wood but only if we're quiet and don't play around. I look through to my house from the dead woods and it looks far away and a lonely place – like the dead woods look from the house. When I found the dead woods I think I noticed that right off. I can't figure out things like that but they stick with me.

Most of the time on the playground I just walk around observing people. I've got lots of friends and we play games and hang out a lot but following people and watching them is fun too. This one kid who saw me following some other kids around came up to me and asked if I was a weirdo or something so I concentrated with my fingers on my temples and told him that I just killed some people in another country, Iran maybe, or Mongolia, just by thinking. Sometimes I feel like I have special powers like that but I usually only use them to make good things happen.

In the woods everything is different and changing all the time. The big trees are always still there though, and the boulders are always in the same place you went by them before. But so much happens when you're not there – it's like I'm in my room and everything outside is changing and getting moved around except those big trees and boulders. Inside nothing changes much though – my room gets messy and I just clean it up – clothes get dirty so they get washed. And inside it's always pretty quiet, but if you open a window you hear all kinds of things going on out there. I wish I could not care if my room stayed messy or I spilled something on the floor. People have to be neat though.

❖

I have a faucet that sounds like a phone ringing behind the sound of water running, and each time I turn it on my heart jumps – as though each time I am again convinced that the phone is now ringing. What does it mean? Whose call do I expect on a phantom phone?

Somebody living above me just laughed – a sly and sinister laugh – so now I'm expecting the phone to really ring...– prank call!

I'm so afraid. I'm so afraid.

❖

Once upon a time a young lad had some last minute Christmas shopping to do so after school he walked down into the old part of town where all the nice shops were. Now this boy had grown too old to believe in Santa so something very strange happened: every time he passed a man dressed as Santa Claus the fellow left off what he was doing and started following the boy! First there was a Santa on a coffee break outside a bookstore – then another one ringing a bell and collecting money for charity – then a third Santa, this one taking young children's Christmas wishes on his lap: "Come back," said the parents of the youngsters, but the Santa just didn't listen.

Well, pretty soon the little boy was being followed by half a dozen Santas. He tried to lose them in an alleyway – he tried to hide from them behind a snowbank – but still they followed, sometimes rubbing their bellies and letting out a jolly "Ho Ho Ho." And then things got worse: a Santa steering a hay cart full of people saw him and started going the wrong way. And then, wondrous to behold, a busload of Santas that happened to be driving by noticed the boy and the bus began following him too! He ran and he ran but every time he thought he'd lost the Santas they'd bumble around a corner toward him – it was terrifying. At one point the boy dropped one of the presents he'd bought but the Santas didn't pick it up, they walked right past it – and the busload of Santas ran right over it! "Oh my goodness," exclaimed the frightened boy.

And then, when he thought he couldn't be more scared something terrible happened: a dead end. All of the Santas on the bus came piling out to join the others and they walked straight toward him. What could he do?! They were getting closer and closer and soon he could see the red in their fat cheeks and the twinkle in each of their eyes – and bunches kept saying "Ho Ho Ho" and then other bunches would say "Merry Christmas" or "Ho Ho Ho" again. Well anyway, the boy just about despaired – the throng of obese merrymakers was nearly on top of him...when suddenly, at the height of his panic, he started to shout. He shouted with all the force his little body could muster. With the stubby hands of a hundred Old Saint Nicks reaching for him all at once he shouted a terrific shout...shouting very loudly now (maybe he was almost out of breath too – perhaps even needed his inhaler). Anyhow, he shouted: "There is no such thing as Santa! There is no Santa! There is no

5

Santa!" And suddenly, slowly – miraculously – the pursuing Santas shrank away, back onto their buses, back to their bookshops and sleighs, their street corners and, for a few, their bottles, until the boy stood alone, shaking and crying but...a man.

And that is the story my daddy told me and his daddy told him and his daddy before that probably heard from somebody else because he was an orphan, and now I'm passing it down to you. And if you still choose to believe in Santa I'll love you anyway. Now goodnight son and "Ho Ho Ho."

❖

If only I could describe this room for you: this Christmas tree and fire, these gifts and knick-knacks, this bundle of wood splintered, speckled with lichen, running with ruts and cracks and grooves. Here are holiday candles out on the mantle and tables – potpourri knocked to the floor by a cat hours ago – and now, Santa's sleigh on the roof! What's it matter if I miss a few particulars, import a fanciful detail?

> In the fire a flank or thigh-piece burning –
> Tomorrow a hecatomb.

❖

Everything I write is from my homemade wooden desk in my wooden shoes, sitting in an oaken chair – is written with a ligneous pencil in a warm log cabin nestled deep in a forest – floats like driftwood freely from me – from the inmost imperturbable cortices of my brain.

1999

For every sad piece of memory I want there opposed, like a battle-steed pricked to charge, some beautiful thing I've lived: Rocinante vs. Bucephalus.[1] Something like that – a rout – and yet, each time the bony nag is trampled o'er, he staggers up again and dodders back to position.

I want to inhabit the boar and the bear, the charger and the hack, the fool and the fool who follows him – both sides, reverse and obverse. There must always be this sidedness...yet always something more. How many lives can be drawn at cross-variance? How many antagonists, how many warring factions, wronged oppressors, would it take to split the stage in twain?!

❖

Infuriating! And why can't I feel more?! I'm so impatient my legs are shaking. It's that stupid time right after the recess bell goes off when you have to put everything silently away, place your folded hands on your desk, and just sit there looking up at the teacher until she reluctantly lets go, "You may be excused." *I want to be excused!*

❖

I back away...I back away and retrace my steps – like that game my brother and I used to play in the woods when there was snow – back to the original path. Sooner or later you can't retrace 'em anymore – you have to stop and hide somewhere or he'll hear you tramping on the snow-covered leaves and brush and twigs. Thank god you're not allowed to cover your tracks, or else you'd never be found out there, even if you were a giant, since you can't make a sound and you can't give yourself away...because what kind of game would it be if you stopped playing it right in the middle? I wish I knew how to stop sometimes – how to quit – but I always had to play it out, or mostly anyway.

I miss those woods I knew so well. There were sticks everywhere, big rocks, little brakes and glades. There was always something falling from a tree: bark chips or leaves or nutshells or fuzz or pine needles, even on a silent, windless day. The forest was alive with activity, but you had to pay attention to notice and appreciate it. And when there was a breeze, it felt like every tree was speaking to you – like every tree was saying something very important, but since so many were talking it sounded confused – doleful. I'd try to piece out what was being said and then I'd stop wanting to listen – it was just too much – but once you've listened for a while you can't stop hearing it, even when you leave...so that now, years later, I still hear it.

❖

Some morning, maybe not tomorrow morning but soon, I'm going to wake up alive – and since we always speak in metaphor really, *tomorrow morning* or *another morning* may just as well end up being in the middle of the day, or near the end of one. But I shall wake up alive sometime, and I have every intention of doing so in the morning hours, or at least that it should appear so. I hope that's clear – what I mean – arbitrariness being what it is.

❖

And still I'm tramping through the woods in my snowsuit going whoknowswhere – just tramping 'til something catches my eye, makes a story, like Frost's bird then woodpile,[2] and I can always watch my breath or break a twig off or eat some snow or make a trail or shake a branch or just fall over and pretend I'm crawling through the snow toward civilization...not gonna make it...but wait! Is that a house?! Oh my god I'm saved! So I jump up and try to run to the door, boots puncturing the icy top layer, down through the powder to the frozen grass and leaves, then thrusting up and out, scattering shards and wedges all 'round.

And I'm alone when I do that, or when I throw snowballs at the icicles clinging to the eaves, or try to skate in my boots down the driveway bumpy with tracks and dirt spots, or dive into the ditch...and by a milkweed get switched.

❖

I wish every piece of sense I ever made came unglued, unhinged, unbolted – dropped down in the muck and mire. Wish I made it all, from now on, with mortar and thatch and adobe and stone and logs – with simple tools too – saving only a single square for a rude pane of glass – or maybe I'll just use clapboards for windows.

But I don't mean it – not all of it there, about rusticating. I do mean that I want people to see – see it all – *me* – me unbalanced, creaking, bent, discolored here and there – clay-footed me.

❖

"Can such things be/ And overcome us like a summer's cloud,/ Without our special wonder?"[3] Must we, then, find a place in the world for horrors and what seem such if we're ever to understand them?

Reminds me of this dream I often have when I nap during the day – not a dream really but...as I slowly open my eyes, directly above me I see a huge arachnoid streaking straight toward my face! Now, every time I awake to this I jump up from the bed and start frantically searching the room – every time – I can't simply swat at the air to prove to myself the thing's not there. I can't, yet as I scan the ceiling and check under the bed, I know there's nothing to be found. This has happened to me five or six times in recent months. And here's the point I'm getting at: by looking for this creature at all I'm trying to find it a place in the world – I'm trying to find a spider bigger than ten tarantulas a home in a corner of my apartment...and for a few seconds at least, I haven't any other choice.

❖

All day yesterday I pined after tomorrow and today, having reached it, I'm only afraid again – afraid for not rushing to write – afraid for not having the one true motive and every damn half o' one I do have embattled and fraught...– and now I think that nobody just sits down and writes or stands up and paints – that it's more like hailing a cab: you're curbside, musing, when second-ly you've urge enough to yell...then down again...more musing...then repeat, 'til the sense of the thing's in front of you, decked out in billboard and check. Better hurry – the meter's running.

❖

Not to know the bottom's there – not to know there isn't bottom – not to be afraid if there isn't. To swim down past shipwrecks and trenches – past them all I say, to where crust meets mantle – to warm me near the core! Or no – to stay here, dry – to find hypercubes in a squirrel's scamper... or in something less contrived.

❖

But there've got to be other, better ways of discerning – ways baffling enough to amaze yet not exasperate – trails steep and precarious, windswept and forbidden... but from which may be heard, however faintly above, a calming sound or kindred murmur – the meditative brook of a Shangri-la – a mountain monastery – a plateau beneath a summit which may or may not be a plateau beneath a summit. Sherpas, base camps, "the shadow of a magnitude"[4] – and the magnitude too!

Tell me I'm not just masquerading in crampons and a parka – that the excitement is real, or the mystery of the excitement – that all may not cohere but there is good reason, meaning behind the dire reaching.

❖

Will not fill my head with their opinions, only sweet ambrosia. Will not let myself be starved out. Never enough! No, not ever, ye catapults and siege engines. Naught is enough 'gainst the mind's portcullis, the infinite concentricities of moats! And I have more – more hot lead and vitriol than all your combinèd host! Always – always there is more *this side* the wall! (Which is to say: I will not read today.)

❖

Hope it rains – I *hear* it raining. Ah, but what good is that? Does drawing buffalo on a wall make 'em real? – Increase the herd? It's soothing is all, magical thinking, so long as no one can see the trick.

There will be a time for such a phrase – *magical thinking* – a time in this *un*dreaming world – a time in the future when hoping it rains *is* hearing it too.[5] But here, on the paper, is magic *now*. Voilà! *I* make it rain, make it heard to be raining: pitter patter on the roofs of cars, pat pat on the even ground – slish along a dandelion shoot, dap upon a clover.

Or do I? Can chirography *achieve* anymore than chalk and ochre? No – it's whether your head believes, not what's in your hand. My head – mine is flat – mind is flat – no Columbus yet – no self-discovery – just Dark Ages methinks...and vulgar superstition, and an acute awareness of underlying uncertainty and insecurity and dread.

❖

If I were silent would I be more pitiable? If the sails were reefed would they catch more wind? Indeed – there's a futility in every gesture of response. So I try too hard – I write too thick and dense – molasses – or maybe just treacle. Yeah, that makes sense: I daub it on.

❖

Quiet day, gray, overcast, cool. It may rain. Yet the breeze on my ankles makes me think of spring...and summer also, sitting on the end of a sandy dock, dipping my feet in and out of the water – of a distant loon in silhouette – a canoe pulled up through bog over roots – a hempen swing dangling, creaking slightly at the staying knot up high over clearness – and the way that clouds move when the same boy passes under them, back and forth, looking out not up, like a pendulum.

❖

Friday – no, Saturday really – it's after twelve. And I've been thinking about it – about writing you a poem...but I just don't have it in me. What *do* I have? Well, to be unblushingly honest I would have to say: gas. But let me tell you, it's no ordinary flatulence – there's something magical in it. Call it effluvium, divine aspiration, kamikaze. Actually, you know – I got it from eating too much manna...or was it ambrosia? I was drunk, I really can't remember very well – there were lots of naked nymphs there though, I think. Whoa, what a party!

❖

When people die part of what you mourn is that they can't keep changing before you – now *you* have to keep them from *not* changing – you have to keep them fresh in your mind, and how is that to be borne? How?! How do you keep a dead person living? Yet you must try.

❖

I say-think-feel-live that I'm getting ready. No, you're not though, even if you say-think-feel-live it – you *are* – you just *are*. There is no getting ready, you're already going and moving and getting there.

Break down – disintegrate – that's more real. *Seem* – no, *sound* – like when a car streaks past and some idiot passenger yells at you and it sounds like "Ahhhbluhhh" instead of what they think you'll hear. It's false – a fraud –

to claim you understand, and something closer to real if you acknowledge you don't. A word, a story, a sound, a moving or stationary image – they're like the ancient toothbrush some archaeologist dug up, plucked outta the dirt and stuck in a glass museum case – matter of fact, every flippin' second that passes is another crusty old toothbrush hardly worth the curator's paperwork cuz there's so damn many of 'em.

    Trying to get to where this makes no sense – where even the hardiest Gnostic scholar gives up the effort to make it cohere. Don't be tricked by familiarities – it never happened to me yet but you could walk up to your cat outside one night and start petting a raccoon. If you think you get it – get it much at all – there's a good chance you're petting a raccoon...which raises a host of health issues.

❖

No more stippling the canvas – no more stopping by to touch up a single dimple or reflection. Broad strokes from now on – broad swathes of brushstrokes henceforward!

If only I had the stories to make it move – all I can do is grind the gears. Yea, 'til the teeth are chewed, 'til the threads are worn smooth.

❖

    If a man came out of the world of my dreams how could he possibly be more bewildered than I am right now... yet he would be – everything would seem so slow here, so hard and unyielding, even almost unrelated – he would find his way of life degraded. Perhaps when we die here we go to live in a place like our dreams where fantastic wonders are the way of things and natural.

❖

    Given a day to write – a whole day with scenery hardly moving – with colors softer than green in the trees – with fading reds and browns and yellows – with a sky more gently pleasing, and light clouds and frosty shade – with Halloween nearing – with piles of leaves – with stacking wood and moss on boulders fading – with rakes and pine cones and the coming wreaths – with special places that do not change – not like the seasons do – or me – because I'm sure I do...though I'd prefer to just lie here awhile not thinking about it, under the raked up leaves, silently, hoping my brother comes along.

❖

    All this thinking – it's nothing – can't help at all with feeling or finding a way. I am alone with myself on a desolate plain. I'm trying to wear a path. Why? I won't be coming back. Will someone else be along this way?
    Why do we remember when it's past necessity? Why do I carry all this history in my head? Every step along the way every prior step has meant a different thing! Now, after so long proceeding, there are just too many reasons why I came – one at least for every day – more even. Set me a path, a straight path right toward the sun – set me one path never changing – push me upon rails – guide me!
    The mystery is on the inside – or that's where it's most urgent anyway – urgent of interpretation and discovery. But it's on the outside too, just the same, a vast carnival with every possible ride and amusement. I stand right now in the midst of the bustling crowd – here's my ticket, "I hold it towards you"[6] – yet, though I can hear

the music and laughter, I *see* only a few garish, shoddy attractions. Above me the shrieks of giddy passengers on storming roller-coasters; nearby the clank of change on iron timbers beneath some whirling upside down sideways transcendental "zipper" ride. All this crazy recondite commerce everywhere around me yet all I can see is the dust of the plain...and, like I said, maybe a cheesy merry-go-round.

❖

Brook crossing – jumping from bank to sandy whorls (sibilant strand – the striations of deposits: illuvial) – over grotto, root, bottom, deep – through the sounding air that spans. Running now, tracing the shore along the other side, down to a little driftwood bridge. Coming back around. Doing it again.

❖

The leaves outside are traveling in so many directions, yet all are as folds in a single sheet of crumpled paper. They gather by the curbside – by, on top of, over. They are like spells and incantations – forces seeking – designs seeking...expression. They scurry over cars and sidewalks, through the interstices of fences, chasing each the stem of the one before it, like dirty little rats freed from a storm sewer. They tumble and skip, are coy. More than this.

❖

I am at once behind and ahead. I am torn through at the present. I am wedged in a fissure of ice!

❖

Tried to move objects, turn my legs into fire, see through and hear through the sanctity of representation. The world also is clay. Form will yield.

❖

When, with metal toothèd rake, a pretty young tenant collects the leaves into one corner of the parking lot in order to diminish somewhat the burden of rent, and another, weed whacker in hand, frees the concrete foundation from the encroachment of stubby hedges – well, then my heart gladdens at the prospect of returning anew unto the living commune which is the workaday world.

2000

There is an old-fashioned sort of bustle, with the plowing and the scraping off of windshields, the sodium-potassium pump in and out of the park. And it is touching to see and hear all the life that first snow brings – all the activity that can't be traced on a page. The light is bronze on the snow – bronze on the airy drifts.

❖

(In response to some philosophical questions put to me)

You speak of a boy in need of instruction. But are we not all children of God? Is not our understanding a child's when we naïvely compare ours to His? We grow through His tutelage. We do not stop growing – as a tree grows toward the sun do we continue to grow toward God.

When I think of God's indulgence – when I sense His beautiful mind rustle, as if it were the single leaf within my hearing – why, then suddenly, quietly, I come to know somewhat a thing I did not know before.

And we grow not only toward, we grow with the power of God – *it* grows *inside* us. I stop and reflect on the long days behind and how different I am – they are as the arms of an embrace that brings more and closer to my heart.

And I may say God did this. God did all these.

❖

When I was a boy I lived near a large lake, and next to the lake was a glassy pond. The pond froze smooth and very dark in winter and in the summer was brown and still next to the blue, breakering lake. And the shore of the lake was a bed of smooth round rocks while the shore of the pond was mud and bits of leaves. I used to throw the rocks out into the choppy waters of the lake and into the stillness of the pond. The lake 'd keep on churning and foaming but the pond would swallow and engulf the rocks. What does that mean do you suppose?

❖

You can't drive a stake into truth – you can't mount it on a pike like the head of a tyrant and wave it over the crowd.

❖

When you find that thing which is infinite a door will open unto you and a light will shine through. And when you speak, at last, that thing most holy and dear to your heart, there will open unto you another door and all the regions of the universe will fill with penetrating silence. And I see a door to boundless calms and one to utter peace. And the hall whence all these issue is an inferno you must walk through and the burning you feel will be real.

❖

Beauty beads up, rolls off, like raindrops gathered on leaves or petals – like mercury in the palm of a boy. The adhesive property binds by artifice not intuition. A pin can float on water. "Aber was ist diβ?!"[7] – A game – a trick – solitaire over and over which, if you win, is of no matter, the game being so fixed to rules and governable.

19

Let a man play at a game he does not know, play it but once, and the game rule him...

I pause...to say a thing more profound. Seems I always have another ace up my sleeve – it little matters: when I was sixteen me and a friend had these two girls over my house and we were all down in the pool room playing strip poker at the bar. Before they got there we'd marked the aces. We lost anyway.

❖

Hardly any snow left now, and that filthy – mostly mud and dirt and grime. Sounds get louder in spring, or near to it – retina brightens also. Seasons, like picture nails, to hang the days on.

Let me say that thing which is infinite – I mean, let me feel the fullest self-expression. Give me words more clear. Make me master of the ineffable. Strike me dumb with wisdom! CONSUME ME IN FIRE!

Everything quivers a little, flickers, and isn't quite real. I need to remind myself of who I am. Is the world a witch that neither floats nor sinks?!

❖

I want to be the Ferryman for a while, poling people over from 'here' to 'who knows where.'

❖

On a dull day leafless trees hang out the earth like roots grown through from the other side. Ah! *This* must be the sterile overworld to trolls.

❖

    I remember water on the leaves, cold, a little later than now, in spring. I remember the ditch at the end of the driveway filled with water, flowing with fineness... of tiny hulls and pollen and leafy detritus and gold dust. How I understood then in a way that seemed satisfactory, still able to gape at the tallness of trees, the flight of birds, the sounds of wind. Pretty thoughts, not a child's per se, but naïve and *of* a child. How I'd throw a ball up over the gambrel roof just to hear my brother say, "I got it." How the lawn dipped and slid away into woods and ferns and baby pines. How I struggled then too, I confess, to discover my equanimity, and never did find it really. I'm so old now compared to then – still lost though – still lying on the lawn looking up at the sky, afraid I'll never *really* understand, and that with the slightest stirring I may float up and be carried away, like a downy feather – like a discomposed thought.

❖

    Observed a woman with barrettes holding her hair back from her face at the comedy club – she scowled at me hard, I guess so I'd feel ashamed.
    No desire except to disappear, such insipidity prevails. Would like to say things hateful...rancorous – rousing anyway. Would like to gather together trinkets enough to constitute a contribution.
    Dreamt I saw a ghost – wasn't sure 'til the man whose father it claimed to be told me his dad's name (which, I remember, was "Rich Day"). Yet I knew it was a dream in that I knew I would be waking. Disappointed, for ghosts would mean there's something.
    It is time again...that something should change.

Seems...seems like people are living their lives. I looked around the room at them all laughing and I got this powerful sense of fuel efficiency. Then I considered myself fidgeting in my seat, distracted and mopey and uneasy, slowing down going up hills cuz my car's lost so much power – the heater not working though the dummy lights still do.

  I thicken up like Daphne turning into a tree...bark spreads over my mouth...and now I'm a tree that bleeds![8]

❖

>Would the waves were higher,
>The surge some splendid inauguration
>Of new flood and drownings.
>Why ride o'er it like a child's top spinning
>'Til the sides tip over – 'til it strike a stone
>Or dart into sand?
>[Pause]
>Leave me to musing – to the cutting breakers
>And swift sea receding – leave me there
>On the glistening ends of oars, back there
>Where just they swirled – farther now, and farther,
>To where the wake is finally forgotten,
>Where shapelessness 's been restored.
>[Pause]
>Ah me – I float on a soundless wake
>That no boat ever made – that only seems
>A wake – really just waves meeting,
>Only seeming to make something new.

❖

What was I made to care for? What was to 've made me passionate more so than another? I take pleasure in nothing. I care not nor strive but to seem to care, when I do not, nor strive. What is my own moreover? – Clothes and a few books – in my head, naught at all. Yet I've struggled on when another might as justifiably have given up and hung themselves with a cord. I am that outcome too, three days undiscovered.

And so my decision is final...as regards caring...of *that* sort anyway: I will surrender my vocation, consign myself to the vagaries of nature, and seek happiness in the canning industry. Hey, it's an honest buck!

Mr. Scad
Dig faster won't you. Hurry up. Get me that old man's head to jab at – get me that moldering dotard's head – yank it off – lemme hear it tear away from 's rotten wormy neck. [hollow sound] Ooooh, what a delicious thud! Go on then Gimmy, put a spade through 's eye – git me down to that gold. Yeah, so never mind the head – never mind that – only let me see it 'fore y' smash it. Hold on now, hold – are you in there? I'm comin' down, hold on. [climbs down] Ah, the perfumes of Arabia.

Bull
There ain't enough room down here.

Gimmy
Hey Bull, look – there's his head.

Mr. Scad
Whoa – somebody fart? Hah! Bull's right, Gimmy – wait up top.

[Gimmy climbs out]

Bull
Screw the head.

Mr. Scad
No, no – yer wrong there – it's not the same – it's not – it's not grave robbin' if you don't smash the bastard's head. There's a procedure here – there's a...oh hell – okay – there – you happy?! Christ Bull, it's all about the money with you. Help me outta this damn hole, Gimmy. Jesus.

[Mr. Scad climbs out]

Gimmy
Uh – the watch – I – did you get the watch?

Bull
Mr. Scad took it.

Mr. Scad
You got something to say to me Bull – is that it?!

Bull
You took the watch.

[Mr. Scad jumps back into grave, presumably onto Bull, a scuffle then a clank]

Mr. Scad
[climbing out again] Greedy sonuvabitch – he'd 'a killed me I think.

Gimmy
He looked pretty mad.

Mr. Scad
Here – take this spade – it might be lucky…Yeah, you think you know a fella then they murder you with a shovel. Reminds me of once when I was real little and I first saw a shovel. Hah!

Gimmy
[quickly refilling the hole] Almost done.

Mr. Scad
And kick over that headboard there – [to himself] he ain't sleepin'.

[Next scene. Same location. Dirt mounded up again next to the hole.]

Magistrate
[covering his nose with a handkerchief] Unholy.

Sexton
Yep – jus' as I 'spected – smashed heads.

❖

Damn parks and greenness – damn laughter among benches and trimmed trees – damn summer coming to all but me who sits apart from seasons in some dank grotto's fetid air, among mushrooms blooming and despicable salamanders.

❖

Behold there, a puffy white stegosaurus bird swimming in the western sky – at least I think that's west – honestly, I'm pretty high.

25

❖

>   Where a high cliff cuts and dives away,
>   Where a great winding stair increaseth,
>   Where the darkness of Design resides –
>   From that fortress wall sees I, in dream,
>   A lady's cap fall. A crow carries it up
>   Into a tree there, and I fly to the tree
>   And carry the cap back down again
>   To the beautiful waiting lady.

❖

Consider how the self evolves without remainder – how precedent gently guides so you hardly know – like a branch that seems meaninglessly to sway through pathless bramble yet you follow and attend.

❖

The gnats that flicker on the surface are me – are what I see – but what on earth is the big fish in the water?

❖

    What's writing when you do not want to write? Or when there's no wisdom in it? What is it when there's some secret thing hiding inside...skulking, mysterious, like a monk on a moor?
    I'm tired out and discouraged...from groping without forward motion...nor saying nor thinking nor feeling a single charitable thing. Suppose I write a piece that describes a violent death – in first person, second, then third, giving words to all the particulars?! But that too would not be enough. I should myself consent to be stabbed i' the throat, or strangled, or gnashed by a tiger.

But it can't come like that either. No – mustn't know it's coming. So – here's some *blood* you demons! [slashes a palm, smearing blood on the page] Now go on – get started!

❖

May it all bewilder, with no categories and no details. May it whisk by, like a Kodiak claw through stream then air. To-live is not e-nough.

❖

This purity of evening makes thinking moot – this hintlessness of day settled like invisible ash on all details.

❖

Don't just write: S*avage the lines!*

Comb and wattle. Beak. Wattle and comb.

❖

  Vampires – they whispered to me last night. I went to close the door of a spare bedroom when, from a latched up loft, I heard one: "Come here." I pulled the door tight and crept slowly away, listening. And I knew, because I'd thought of them – imagined they might be there – that now, certainly, they would be, even if they hadn't been before. I was very afraid, and very much awed by fear, by the demons fear can summon. Why do I hope I may dream of them again?

❖

Because I want to be so famous that hills grow out of my head and grass and bleating sheep, then prophets dressed as shepherds and not even yet prophetic nor named in scripture.

❖

I want to write about it – about how wonderful she was – the way she smiled at me there, lying on her side, knowing who I am. But then the dream turned, like milk does – I knew it was turning when it did – and I simply let the rest go by, no longer caring, because she was gone and I was just someone alone.

❖

So I'm kinda drunk a little, I don't care – I'll debauch this book just the same. It ain't Prohibition anyways...so leave me alone yah teetotalers – guardians of the establishment. Yeah, I've g't nothin' to say – so what!? What's that got to do with it?! I can dress this drinkin' up nice like you know, but that's no fun really. Drinkin's about bein' exaggatory 'n loud all over the place. I only wish I wasn't sittin' around this table here alone – laughin' at nobody 'cept maybe myself.

❖

I need something to take the edge off
Maybe a Popov or Stoli or Smirnoff
A shot of vodka to kill the pain
Or something metal I can aim.

❖

Since wanting to write sentiments darker than pitch I've diminished somewhat to the soaking rat now squeaking before you. Or am I a serpent? A mole? A seahorse? I'm protean sure – daren't pause within the skin of an instant!

❖

In a book about Heine there's an epigraph at the head of a chapter admonishing the reader to avoid deep inquiries into the lives of artists and just settle for the beautiful products of their lives...cuz if you look too closely the beauty disappears and you'll see how these self-styled *poets* actually crawled out their lives on the dirty, sweaty earth like common earthworms (you know: Lumbricidae family, class Oligochaeta). Anyway, it bugged me. Am I wormin' around leaving mucous trails when I'm not fleshing out the beautiful ideas in my head or some bullshit like that?! I don't know – I'm confused – but maybe I want to show that I'm an Annelid poet – that I'm the blind Homer to the whole wriggling phylum. It ain't pretty, is it – makes you squirm – but doesn't that squirmin' just prove that you too are a slimy worm? And besides, it's not as if I talk about eating dirt and shitting dirt all the time. Or do I? Oh dear. You know, I lost my point – how embarrassing. But that's okay...cuz I'm the Annelid poet and I can do that! I can do anything!

Yippee! – Annelid Poet – Yahoo! Now I won't feel so bad when people say I'm too annelidic. And if someone asks me, "Are you a bookworm?", I won't bristle my setae and make a snide remark – I'll stand up tall and say, for all to hear, "Yes, I am!" (That is, if bookworms are Annelids – I've got people researching this.)

Remember – so much is left out. Silences, reticences. Why? I don't know but that's just how it is and no escaping.

Nevertheless, I am the Annelid Poet, and all my segmented brethren speak through me in one united voice!

❖

These books and pens and papers:
Armaments strewn o'er the sodden floor of my field tent.

❖

Two city workmen
Spirit the leaves
With gas-fired hoses

A woman
Waiting for the bus
Demurely observes.

❖

Fucking snow scalded away by bitter rain, by poison dripping down on the innocents' foreheads, tormenting – torturing – as doth this pallor creeping o'er my skin: drained the life therefrom, desiccant the flesh-soaking rain rain.

Wish I had it fixed in my mind, the idea – be it suicide or some monomania – anything that'd keep me whole when perishing.

Wish I could burn alive every woman and man – blight the cheek of every child...so that they too would be as I.

Wish I could block out the sun at every pique or peccadillo – just stab someone through the head who's walking down the street – yea stab the dog they're walking too, laugh, lick the blood, then say one o' them dumb macho things Achilles always said.

I am the murderer – I admit it – it was me – I killed 'em all...ate their hearts.

Think that maybe I'll go on a Christmas rampage. Ah! You will say that I'm splenetic. So is the wind! Santa, I cast thee out!

❖

(Christmas email sent from work to friends)

I been thinkin' about this whole chad thing 'n it put me in mind of them poor old C.H.U.D.'s reachin' up 'n grabbin' people by the legs cuz they're so lonely.[9] And I thought, "What would I do if I was a Chud on Christmas?" And I started to feel very sad, sad for all them rancid-faced Chuds scrapin' at the windows of us more fortunate, recognizable humans, wishin' they could eat roasted goose-flesh...wishin' that they knew how to roast or cook or even chew really. Chuds don't have churches or soup kitchens or support groups – all they've got is air vents that might blow some warm industrial pollutants onto their frostbitten scabby old claws.

Oh Woe, Woe to all the Chuds in this cruel cruel world – life dealt the Chuds a crappy hand – maybe a pair of fours – and they gotta play it even though they don't know how.

There's a Chud in all of us yearning, yearning to be free of chudliness.

God bless you Chuds – God bless you everyone!

❖

How 'bout a voice not yet heard from – one that more calmly surveys and attends to life, unafraid of ordinaries, whether dusty or clumped together or brick-hard with frost – one that trails off in a whisper and never is heard from again. R.I.P. eternally.

❖

Ice-skinned stream remember
When as a boy
Roots and spills and mossy deadwood
Caught clear pools for dreaming.

2001

Nightmares, more or less, several times in the last week, which I take to be a goodly omen...

In one of them some force or spirit conducts me through a house that seems vacant...but no – I'm afraid of something – something lonely and forbidden and awful going on. As we move through the rooms, one by one, the doors swing open before us and we get closer and closer, until finally we come to a door that's shut – I'm terrified by now – and then slowly it opens: a child is cowering in a corner next to the toilet – a woman in front of him shields us from view. What is she doing to him?! – Something satanic – mutilating his soul – tearing it out of him – choking him – suffocating him with unspeakable nearness.

In the other I wake up at home very early in the morning, having heard something downstairs. I creep down quietly: nothing. But it feels cold...like a window is open. I turn out of the hallway into the living room. Oh God! There *is* a window *wide open* the screen out curtains billowing – now I'm sorry I was so quiet – should've made more noise. I hear a slight creak and turn slowly toward it – a figure is there, towering in the dark, waiting to be seen.

Maybe they mean my mind is moving. Then welcome hag and welcome horror, I will love thee both together.[10]

At the trial of a bread roll the pigeons pass judgment. The sentence, unwrit in their English, one can only infer: "death by minute consumption." But wait! Halt the execution! This crow has something to say on the baguette's behalf. Step forward Mr. Crow. Order! Order I say! Bailiff, call the court to order. Bailiff, stop picking at the defendant! Oh the horror!

❖

When I dream tonight I shall become conqueror of all the kingdoms near me. Then, having subdued them, I'll go out of my castle to live among the vanquished. And the castle will become a garden of ivy and a play yard for children and a nesting place for birds.

❖

Do you wonder where song inheres
What sings the breeze
The paths among trees
Tunefully along?

I'm trying to identify the mystery that makes the morning move so. I cannot find words. I am a roaming herd led somehow by the hindmost lagging calf.

❖

If I am, right now, all of my possible futures, then allow me to apologize if this doesn't turn out so well. It may be that I shall be struck by a plow, or lose my mind, or worse yet, 'never amount to much.' But you must bear in mind that I have, er, *had* the very best intentions, and would've preferred – if I don't get one, that is – a *happy* ending.

Please remember, it is often difficult to coax a climax or crisis, even when the story really needs one – especially when that story happens to be your life – and getting the right sorts of characters to make appearances at opportune times – introducing a romantic interest, for example, providing foils and counterplots – can be darn near impossible. It's a learning experience for me every day, and I'll be honest, if I had it to do over there are a few things I would change – certainly I would seek an advance.

❖

> Wonder closes
> With ornate vents
> With diaphanous folds
> Windless now

The fan. No – does not work – I force anything at all – anything. It's like I'm a giant trying to furnish a little girl's dollhouse...breaking a couch in my fingers, upsetting a table, losing tiny forks.

❖

> Cold like the dark is
> Cold like harrowing dark
> Cold like black boughs
> Cold restless with evening
>
> Insuperable cold
> Chilling a young boy's shoes
> While he skates, skates on,
> Rīvening.

❖

> Awaken you motes in my eyes
> A new day invades us
> Will contest even
> The smolders of our bivouac!

❖

    It's not the wretched humility imposed by our total aloneness on a forlorn clod but rather, the utter unlikelihood of rescue from blissless ignorance, that makes scribbling and suing for world peace both seem equally absurd. Matter of fact, if someone ground up all the energy of creation right now and put it in a pill I don't even think I'd eat it. Provoked enough by scorn perhaps, I think I'd feed it to my cat, 'n let him take over day to day operations down here...on planet clod.

❖

Like any other sot I just wanna know: Am I wrestling with an angel or anachronism?

❖

    Be all this as it may, or may not, because I care not, disavow all such efforts, emprises – my place is assured, for I am my own recognized species much like whales are or slime molds. I have my own niche to fill in the Anthrosuperskilodgical record and be damned if I won't fill it! Don't mind if I do, thank you very much, step aside ladies. Yes yes, that's right – yes, it's me the taxidermist's come to classify – I'm uncharted territory – I'm a livin' and breathin' wunderkind right outta Area 51 or the North Pole or the dark side of the moon. One of a kind baby – Yeah! – Outta sight!

...Don't matter – no, it don't. I can stretch it out from yesterday to tomorra but it'll snap back taut again soon as I let go. Yet I know know *know* if I could just get a little rip or tear goin' maybe we'd all get sucked in but maybe, maybe somethin' new 'd happen.

But let's pretend I did not stop – that I kept right on talking through the night and into today and evening once again – that you've been ill and I've been sitting at your bedside all the while trying with words to make you well. Or that I'm a spirit floating in the air of an orchard where you read, floating like ripest apples do. Or the soul of a mountain spring, or the genius of some river ford, or...I cannot say...

Will I be nothing? Am I nothing? Put your cheek to the page gentle lady – restore me – make me whole again. How can it be?! The page it stays the same – the words reread unread their meaning. What is left? You are – I am – distant as a million ages without direction.

❖

A postman passed by me today on my walk home from work: "Dontcha love this weather?" "Yeah, really," was my all-squinty-bundled-up acknowledgement-slash-reply, then I got a few steps farther down the hill and thought, "Yes, I *do* love this – the snow falling seems like meaning." And now, sitting in my rocking chair listening to *Rosamunde*,[11] I record the splotchy, prickly sting of the snow then and what that postman said and what I replied and thought.

❖

This breeze right now is like ten breezes before it – I could even enumerate them – yet which one particularly, or is it all? The sun will set soon and I'll pack away thinking again for days. Seems the chimneys are facing westward in stoic reverence. On one side only or parts of two their faces are alight. And the windows on the western sides of houses also are adoring.

❖

...And now the chimneys are squinting their sooty crenellated eyes, for it is midday, the sun as yet unchastened.

❖

>Green a green so green
>It's hardly yearing
>In jade green trees
>
>So green the greens
>Are shadow leaves
>In jade green trees
>
>Shadow leaves like
>Embers burning
>
>Shadowy embers
>Hardly yearing, burning
>In jade green trees.

❖

Asked a coworker if she'd go to a wedding with me – I did not discompose her in the least, though *it* surely did *me*. I am certain I must be too much for her...because I am willing to take risks, though I trip over myself and come off oafish. Really, today, in asking her I lost my poise – something that doesn't much happen to me. And this young lady – she's a touch icy...and I would do better *not* trying to bend my meager heat lamp on emotional igloos. Yet...yet under the parka and sealskins she's a tender lass: "Come out of your ice hut my Inuit queen, that I may regale you with shark tooth necklaces and lichen bouquets! Hey! Hello...?? Alright, I'll leave them outside...I'm going now...Goodbye...Bye..."

Never mind the conceit J. – I adore you.

❖

Long IM conversation with J. tonight – her coyness is devastating though I am not at all susceptible. Doesn't matter, I may be smitten just the same.

❖

Walked with J. yesternight, then she showed me her place and we sat on a couch and tried to 'be with' each other, two feet apart. I think it was a make-out couch – it bore all the signs. She is very sad – sadder than me – because she feels so much more than she lets reach the surface where, from time to time, a fragment or artifact bubbles up and bobs in the current, until urgelessly borne away.

We had a nice walk and I wanted desperately to throw her in the bushes – you know, grab her – but I just mumbled about next to her the whole way.

❖

WARNING: Extreme arbitrariness to follow.

So last night we went all over then came back and watched her favorite movie, then   ,   ,   -   , and   for a period of time by which I shall henceforth

39

measure all earthly intervals, not to mention its factoring into any quantum, meteorological, and/or seismic calculations I may choose to undertake. And whether that makes complete sense or seems a bit elliptical, mind my opening caveat.

I am so unhappy besides though – I don't want to use up my time with her. Every day I expect some nameless approaching imminent forfeiture to snatch away this unnameable immanent beautiful gift. Will there ever be peace in my mind?

Cruddy prose, sticking out sideways, you shoulda been there – I'd 've laughed at your withering – poetry even was not admitted – there were just two.

❖

Flowery spaces
Follow me
Fill me in

And remember for me
Pretty places
Where I've been.

❖

I perceive that it is all a cycle, albeit a "widening gyre," and that there is no *only* escape – that creativity, for me, is a streaking secant, an unretiring unhorizoning boundlessly straight line progression toward and through the falcon's tiny spirals.[12]

❖

What I know about. The things I understand. Now that the leaves have passed. Dimly, apperception. The crowns of trees have two buds – two racemes – a stalk that climbs and a stalk that dies – a stalk that bes and a stalk that seems. Across the street, in cracked cement, a Laurentian staircase flows, turgid with leaves.[13] I am embarrassed at not having a subject or a crown – no capitals for my temple.

❖

Cloud-moving shape like a manatee: Beware of motor-boats in the sky!

2002

(Emailed home from work)
Subject: Text-iles

     Caught myself looking for something I wrote (I'd written) – didn't matter what – enough to circumscribe this tortured hour with – some little piece of lace or filigree. What for? To keep me in mind of...of what I said to Jennie...and how it needs to be. Am reminded of all the nifty swatches piling up – the patterns and arabesques. Maybe I'll make a quilt! Let's remind myself – 'sending'...

❖

How I struggle to surface – like a suffocating whale beneath a wide, dense floe – like a dying man whose lungs feel hugely, malevolently pressed upon.

My gawky pen stumbles into synonym, pitches headlong over synecdoche into a stream of self-consciousness.

❖

    When I say you
    Before I speak
    When first I felt
    Ah what you are
    Possesses me.

❖

That I could burst from my clothes,
    A raging spirit,
    Storm over seas
That I could gaze with gigantic eyes
    On galaxies and tiny seeds
That I could create and uncreate
    Die and be born again
    Never end and end
That I could step outside myself
    Inhabit leaves and stars and things which can't be seen
That I was not bound by modesty
That I could make this body disappear!

❖

I cannot think but I reel
Nor understand even
These tiny words
But for the pain that they occasion
And the confusion
And the exquisite life
They cannot bring me
Nor hope to
Because you do
Mortal loving you
Beautiful you.

❖

Black shadows
That's what leaves are
And branches
And my own profile
Across the sidewalk
On this night without end.

❖

    Corked my ears, though it's not cork really, so that now I'm sitting below, at my captain's desk, in the stern of a delicate ship-in-a-bottle. Call her the *Armada* – she's a galleon for sure, laden with all the tiny treasure a hobbyist could tweeze into her hold. She's like to me, I think, and where I've been. She's like to the millions of high seas adventures I'll never 've been a part of – or to the millions of shipmates and savages who for all eternity will 've come before and after.

    Why are there so many many men, even inside of one? Why are there so many more coordinates than any one man, or many, ever may sail toward? Whither the clouds? Aye, wither 'em – shred 'em with grapeshot me hearties! Knock the wind right outta 'em!

    Will this be my only log?! Swear – swear on a doubloon – swear on the queen's bloody treasury we'll find a way off this mantelpiece, even if it means we shatter on the hearth stones, or find ourselves marooned in a tinderbox.

    Ourselves? There's only me! And there's no boat or log or bottle. And why swear...? If there was only some guarantee that I might live awhile and determine *myself* 'whether or not' and 'what I might' and 'how it came to be.' I just cannot pretend it makes sense or that there's time enough or benevolence.

    Give me a metaphor I can't steer 'round – that envelops like air, not glass!

❖

    Let me emphasize the incidental nature of this inquiry. Yes, it's true, I hadn't the least inkling to write, it's just that the computer database I use to do my job is down at the moment, leaving me – incontestably the quotidian me – standing alone next to my cubicle with nothing else to do...

Oh jeez – Jennie came along and spoiled things – now there's a tense to work with, and an episode. Just doesn't seem the same. Strange. Words...

Wait...– it went away – the feeling of purpose I mean – I'm genuinely unwriterly again. Welcome, my friends – welcome to this brief period of quiescence – this brief eight hour interval in each weekday. Why do they call 'em *weekdays* anyhow? Ah, the life. Should I be concerned that I am here so much – that so much time is utterly lost to a merely remunerated industry? I suppose.

❖

>Water pools in the plastic chairs
>Of summer dreams
>Grooves the lunch break pavement edge
>Musses hair and dress
>Oozes through all concern.

❖

>The old rain falls out of trees
>The rain from yesterday
>Still remembered
>This freshness of morning
>
>Gazing upward still
>Now summoned down
>By the currents of days
>To stop remembering.

❖

Winter '93-'94 living off campus – I'm lying in bed upstairs in my tiny room. It's 2:30 in the morning and I can't sleep because the stereo's turned way up down in the living room where two or three drunk friends are still making noise. "Oh, What a Night" is playing and Frankie's going on about some groupie from way back, though he doesn't tell us much, except that she was good. I lie there for a while thinking about what's significant in the moment. Really, I'm just getting frustrated that I can't get to sleep, but they're not worried about that at all down there – they're still having a good time when most of the rest of us are unconsciously floating toward morning. And there are all these layers to what's happening and the night and it doesn't seem like I'll ever quit worrying. No. So I climb down from my loft, go around to the top of the stairs and yell for them to please be quiet. Then I go back to bed, realize what I've made of a single circumstance, and the resignation puts me out.

❖

The way the world is
Trying to make you feel like you fit
I've experienced it sometimes
Who knows if it's real.

❖

I'm ashes now and probably have no spirit – I'm just these words. I hate th't that's probably true – I hate that there's nothing for me to believe. I hope that there is for you. I hate that we cannot know each other here, in this world, but that we must wait and die to discover the truth...– I mean, whether we shall meet. I cannot think that we will. I'm sorry. I hope I'm wrong. I do hope. Because I want to know everyone and I want to believe in wonderful things.

❦

Went apple picking today with Jennie and her five year old niece, though the day was unusually warm and didn't feel quite right for it. And the rows of the orchard seemed inhospitably long and deep, and the terrain very unmeadowy despite the luxuriant whorling grass – rugged and uneven, so that one walked with plodding difficulty. And the scent of apples was there, in essence, as was the poem of Frost. And the higher trees outside hemmed us in – the people and apples and weekend industry – with sorrowful whispering shadowy device. We took a ride in a hay wagon down along the side and I felt sure something was in that place, above us perhaps, gripping the scene, peering in like it was a plastic snow globe.

I don't feel like I matter at all. I don't feel like there's a voice inside that can slow the brawling crazy momentum long enough so I can write any of it down, make it make sense – not without mixing metaphors anyway, committing a thousand heresies of opacity and ambiguity. And, should I say it clear, would it even *mean*? There isn't a thing we're born to that's verifiable.

Have I had "too much of apple-picking?"[14] Yeah – I'm gettin' tired of thinking, and it ain't just the apples. The different shapes – the figures of the day – the different, the contradictory sympathies – the confusion.

I am nothing. I am nothing.
I am nothing. I am tremendous.

I'm a wild colt. I'm bust loose o' my stall! I'm tearin' through that awful fuckin' orchard without a thought in my head, bursting apples with my hooves, snapping down branches full of 'em – galloping hard up the driveway, bolting suddenly over a rock wall – gone into the forest on quick redolent feet.

❖

Whether Monday mornings mean more deeply introspective is a matter for conjecture. To me, I think it would not matter much what day came first in the week, I'd still feel the same solitary kinship with the gloom outside that day – I'd still feel like beginning and ending, like change is underway in some remote corridor of Nature. Somehow the air is more clear, a gull's wing beats more discretely, a stapler is more dew-cold to the touch, on Mondays. Whatever it is that so makes ideas cling to objects, they are sound ideas, and they seem real objects – together, both have majesty. Mondays.

❖

What is to be said? I begin each day with "What is to be said?" Nor does that new day seem ever to even minimally relieve or redress the ache of the question, the numbness of the bewildering interrogatory. There does not, I confess, present itself, a way out of the design.

Will I perish utterly? Will I pass away to somewhere else? Will I trail truth in my cerements as I stride toward the grave?

I hate to talk like I have not been – I want the words to reach as fingers do and hands.

I'd hate to be read like a musty book – I want the words to rise like bread does from the kilny page.

Live. What does it mean to live? Why do we make for ourselves tiny mysteries? Behold! Black-robed, murmuring, acknowledging *it* is out there – more than one – levering dark truth into the universe, little by little, sacramentally.

❖

We were high that evening, Pat and Eric, Ryan and I. We walked down Meetinghouse Hill while it snowed and snowed through the still air. Everything was white. And it was so quiet you could hear the flakes fall: "sssss." We laughed out warm breath. In the park at the bottom of the hill the icy pond was covered in snow. We swept it away with our boots until we'd cleared a chute. Laughing still and smoking cigarettes, we ran and slid, ran and slid, in the bright snowy light, like children.

The gazebo nearby was lit up, and the wooden bridge over a neck in the pond. Holiday lights festooned the trees. It was past eleven so the traffic signals were blinking yellow, silently blinking. It felt like the world was ours. We smoked some more pot I think and drifted homeward, back to Pat's basement, to drink soda and play video games and listen to music. The laughter issued quietly into reverie. I remember smiling, slumped over on his couch, watching Pat blow those perfect smoke rings. I was eminently satisfied with an experience. I did not wish for more.

❖

All the elisions which constitute loss. The bowdlerizing principle that keeps us from ever becoming whole, or wholly real. Tedious, perfunctory, pedestrian by turns.

I remainder only what vague sense deems especially *this* or *that*, rather than merely. I let go veracities, cut 'em and truncate. I present an exquisite portrait of a...a...uh...a charming depiction of...ahem...– but perhaps I'll just touch it up a bit more first.

❖

It must be *Big Fall* today, so many leaves are coming down and winds are blowing out. And the sky is so blue. I remember the way blue sky looked when I was alone, walking the paths through the woods, seeing it ahead above a glade, wondering where it tended. What does the blue do? Where will it lead me to? Eternity for me may involve a lot of walking those paths again, trying to figure out what they mean still.

It's only when a leaf finally hits the ground that you see it shudder a little – the whole way down is a dance. Chasing the leaves – catching them – crumpling them in the hand – I wish I knew how I learned from that. There's just no understanding.

❖

Some days – mornings, like these – the illusion persists. I type away as Jennie chats on the phone. Great civic projects flit through my mind, inventions, the founding of institutions! Perhaps I'll build a tree house equipped with light and heat, a rope ladder you can pull up, and a hammock on the roof – or I'll charter a whole community of 'em just for the homeless with no one else allowed up except squirrels and social workers.

There aren't any robins left on the lawn, just twitching leaves. Long shadows and more icy blue skies. This has been an unmellowing autumn.

I want to get out of here. I want to make day trips to gorges and caves, walk along age-old trails, stand under a stone bridge out of the rain. I want to be alone – totally alone. Or I don't want to. Where shall I go? There is nowhere to live on this earth. Nowhere for Pericles.

❖

> A warm-sick feeling clots my neck
> Is there a place where we can be
> The threatening crimson won't come out?

❖

You know how the school bus sounds when it's the only thing coming on the road and you're standing there at the stop just waiting? Maybe before you heard it you were throwing snowballs or whipping the ground with a stick, but then you heard it, faraway, and now it keeps getting louder and louder as it comes up the hill, until it rumbles around the corner at the bottom of the street so you can finally see it and you know you're scared but you don't know why. Well, that's how it is with me, only the bus never gets all the way here, it just keeps coming and coming.

❖

Up in a tree behind our apartment I think there's a giant cocoon hanging. It wasn't there last week. And now I wonder, should I ask the neighbors about it or will they think I'm nuts, tell me it's just a bunch of branches? I've been watching it for a few days and it's stayed pretty much the same, swaying a little maybe, but the thing is ten feet long so if it *is* a cocoon or chrysalis or something there's gonna be trouble soon. How is it nobody saw the monster caterpillar anyhow? Creepy.

❖

> Last night as you sleepily murmured
> And wrenched the blankets away
> I laughed at your beauty
> A low and giddy laugh
> I could not quite control
> And I want you to know
> I've never laughed like that before
> Never felt so human and loved.

❖

Can't manage to keep a diary proper or I'd 've said a few things before now about Mom's best friend dying, and Thanksgiving come and gone, and how the story cannot renew itself anymore and so has dropped like a picture book from a child's hand into a beat-up wooden toy box at the end of his bed. He slams the lid down just to hear the slam and smell the wood whoosh. "What's going on up there?!" He comes out onto the balcony above the living room and looks down over the banister at Mom, who's probably reading a paperback, or just sitting in a chair, smoking and sipping a glass of Coke between chores. "I don't know," he says, "I'm bored." "Well why don't you go outside then?" "Yeah, I guess so." He shuffles slowly down the shag-carpeted stairs and makes his way through the dining room and kitchen to the cold breezeway, where his snowsuit's hanging up and his squashy moon boots are. Outside now, he tromps straight out over the yard and tumbles down a slope into the woods. There's new snow everywhere around him, even on the thinnest branches, and the air is completely still. He lies there on his back for a while just taking it in, then senses something – Mom, watching him from a window – so he gets to his feet, climbs back up to the yard, and suddenly, rather anxiously, runs across it to the woods on the other side, out of her view.

And what's there? – Oh, I remember...but am I really gonna fill this out with more detail? The 'grandfather' tree – a giant white pine – out past the hemlock. The rest were poplars I think, and maple saplings, though there was a thick birch near the corner of the house. Trees. Maybe he'd lean against the trunk of the grandfather tree and gaze up at it with his chin on the bark. He'd often think, even much later on, about the tallness of that tree, about its always being there.

I'm playing my favorite Christmas CD as I write this, *A Winter's Solstice IV* by Windham Hill artists. When we were all still alive Christmas music played almost nonstop through the holidays. Mom particularly liked carols sung by the Mormon Tabernacle Choir or Vienna Boys' Choir – I've got some on the hard drive. And we had these green and red decals of reindeer and stars and trumpeting cherubs that my brother and I would stick on the sliding glass doors while the caroling went on behind us.

Walking in the woods filled with snow is like being the one person in the world Nature talks to – I know I've said that before. But who is Nature? What is the natural way? I detect no mystery now – nobody – nothing. Was it all, even then, secretly empty to me?

He walks further out into the woods, away from

the grandfather tree toward the rock wall, then over it to a path. The path leads wherever he will go. He goes up, up through the afternoon December sky. He never comes back down.

❖

After she died I kept listening to the answering machine tape, over and over, over and over, trying to memorize her voice. And I think that now, if she did speak to me, I would definitely know who it was...but she won't. She won't. Maybe my brain is like that tape and it's been demagnetized. Maybe I'm like that Nixon tape science is bringing back – maybe *I* can be brought back, what do you think? I wonder what happened to that little machine tape. I wonder what happened at all.

It's like a train wreck you know, it really is, just like they say, only not just her dying but the whole thing, the whole damn thing. Why? Cuz the tracks just seemed to end, like we should've known all along they were going to. I wish I could set that train back on again and do it all over, really I do, because now, after, nothing feels as real – I'm not a part of anything the way I was.

I can hear her talking up there in my head, asking Dad things during dinner with it all quiet and the living room dark behind us so that I was even a little afraid of the dark there and the quiet – what they meant. She'd ask him about things outside, past the yard and the woods – about unfamiliar people and places I did not know – they were strange questions.

❖

I hate the way it feels sometimes, walking home, when you know it won't feel much less lonesome to get there, *where* you're going. How can it ever 've seemed so? Maybe it doesn't for most – you get there and you're still alone really. Or maybe not – who can say. But I've felt that way so many times...as I've been crossing a street or cutting through a park. I've thought about my eagerness and just *who would care* whether I got home, now, later, ever. Sooner or later no one will – no one will even know. Whole histories of men have been lost.

One raw day I walked over to the university library from my apartment. I didn't know what I was gonna read so I just cruised the aisles grabbing this or that, sampling, 'til I came to a book on Cook's adventures, and I sat down with that 'til I'd read how he died.[15] It sickened me, but that was something at least – briefly there was danger in my humdrum day. I left a little after – I guess I'd had enough. Out in the cold again I thought something like this: "Even though I'm pretty sure I'm not gonna get killed that way, walking on the sidewalk is sort of like being on foreign shores – maybe so is being at home. And not only that, but it's practically a dead certainty everything sooner or later 'll be forgot."

❖

Sometimes I just sit and gaze at my writing, thinking about who it must've been concocted the stuff and what, if any, relation he might bear to me, his poor successor. And then, maybe I lean forward in my chair a little and change a word, or I hear a bird singing or a memory's called to mind and I start adding a something on to the end, tentatively at first, but then, with increasing confidence, expanding it and adding some more, 'til it begins to grow and grow, more and more rapidly – growing now like the Grinch's heart does as he tugs at his sleigh! And then it's *off*, bounding away, cavorting like a young buck in a high snowy glade, prancing around, charging at who-knows-what, delightfully, defiantly, making his stand.

2003

"Where does it come from?" They ask me that. Well, no, they don't, but if they did I'd tell 'em. I'd tell 'em it comes from somewhere deep down, somewhere really deep, like a well, only in my brain. Yeah, and you'll need to crank that pail straight to the bottom if yer gonna fill it, cuz I'm in a drought right now.

Used to be it came from curiosity and confidence, I think. Used to be I had somethin' to say on almost any subject 'cept maybe the weather cuz there's nothin' more tedious than small talk about the weather. Yep, used to be – now all I've got is how bitterly cold or pleasantly mild it is today or was yesterday and hope tomorrow turns out better than the forecast because did you notice that's been happening a lot lately, though I guess it was more spring-like last year 'round this time...

I wonder if I'm finally empty of ideas like I am of hope – or maybe both are spilling out of that pail as it comes up.

You know, I like wells. We didn't have one when I was a kid but I remember looking down into the septic tank once before it was emptied, wishin' I had a penny to drop, thinkin' hard about all the mystery down there swishin' around with the feces. Nowadays I'd prob'ly jump in a sewage treatment vat if I thought it'd make any difference at all – if I thought it'd give me somethin' more to talk about than the weather. I guess it would. Raw sewage usually is good for a laugh.

❖

Ah, but who will ever know "the burning and the strife"[16] – or the slog of the employee – the lost languorous hours – the multitude of interruptions? Who will ever know the...the...the excuses?

❖

They are outside. They are walking on the grass. What do they want?

"Oh, my God," I heard – muffled panic – through the basement ceiling, while I was down doing laundry.

In a dream a man keeps taking off suits of clothing, taking them off, taking them off, until he takes off the last one, and disappears.

I was playing baseball yesterday.

Power is still on. Reed in his chair. Jennie at class.

Someone's knocking.

No wait – she's back early. They're gone.

Tried to scare myself up into a craze thinking about the fear of endings...and fearing them. On the drive home from work I thought of a way to bring the thread back through – lost it though then – almost blunk out.

❖

The rain. Jennie drove us through it to a shopping plaza with a video store and I'll be damned if I let a single thing disturb my reverie...cuz you gotta let life happen sometimes and not try to fill it up every chance you get.

Rain was falling all over the parking lot as I strolled the strip mall colonnade for hours while Jennie shopped – or a few minutes anyway – a few minutes rich with reflected stanchion light and SUV sssspprassshing over wet tarmac. Or do we call it tarmac here? – I can't remember – I'm still in a rainy reverie, a damp do-nothing dream.

You know, I never do keep going long enough – long enough to draw you in. There's all this other *stuff* out there in what I saw and felt and heard – why can't I bring a little more of it to bear? Here – I'll try:

Thought of the rain there, slanting in the light, whether it was beautiful – whether I thought it so. "I'm not sure what beauty is anymore," I observed, but it did not alarm or chagrin me really, it just made me feel, as usual, that change is underway. "I'm not sure that rain falling on blacktop, or even somewhere else, is what I mean by beauty anymore, or what I think of, anyway, as beautiful. Can something like rain falling always be beautiful? Can anything always be something else, anything else, other than itself?" And then I walked past a column in front of a pharmacy and thought of Roman villas, because I think they had colonnades sometimes, either outside or along the atrium. They were pretty random thoughts, probably not at all Latinate, but I thought about how rain falling in a parking lot connected me to them, the Romans – I mean, I didn't explicitly say that to myself, but the idea of it was in my head, and what it meant about time and human history...and even, I suppose, about rain.

Well, we did rent a movie – *High Noon* – so I guess that'll have to do for now, but I got a little more in – tried a different angle. Hope it helped.

❖

I thought I saw a friend before me
He was shrieking in a mask
For he could not breathe
Nor see through the eyeholes
And his face was hot with suffering
I went to where he was
And tried to soothe him
But he was already far gone.

❖

I talked to Grammy last night – she was sitting near the entrance of a bazaar. Her hands were more leathery than I remember but her health seemed much improved. I was surprised to see her – in fact, at first I walked right past her – but when I realized who it was I came back and took her hands. Then I was sobbing as she smiled on me, much less beakèd than in life, much less bitter. I did not ask her how she was. I did not ask her about Mom or Grump. I asked her only what I knew I must have time to ask: "What does it mean?" Her face deeply saddened, as if she had already some notion what my question would be: "I don't know anymore than you do," she said, conveying humility, gravity, and wonder.

❖

If I read one more flight data recorder transcript I'll give up all hope there's anything but death when I die. The last word of every captain is "shit" and "oh my god" comes right before that. Earlier today I was walking back to my cubicle when it occurred to me that I'm just a delicate little organism with some brains near the middle –

and now I'm thinkin' it's jello I meant – that we're all like little jigglin' cubes of jello with a coupla toothpicks stickin' out for legs. What are those people that bruise easy? Well, we're *all* like them, only most of us just don't have it quite so bad. Now I know what the holier-than-thou's mean by "sublimating the flesh" – I think I know what the fuckers are getting at, and yeah, they gotta point: you take off, bank hard to the right, crash near a hangar, and explode in a ball of flames – being jello is like that.

How's it explain the kid in the background though? – The one yelling "Daddy!" Doesn't – not one bit. See, bein' jello is one thing, but kids suffering – I don't have a metaphor for that.

I also don't have much in the way of plagues to rail at, or famines, or pogroms...but when a plane crashes here they post what the people on it said – they put it on the internet and transcribe it in the news – so I know – I know how it is. I know how bad it can get. And, you know what? I know besides. I know without all that... because it's May 20th, the day you died.

"Ah, but what about AIDS and terrorism, what about al Qaida, what about complacency?", I start thinking, making myself feel awfully guilty because I like the ending I had and I don't want to change it. Look – a body's gotta be left alone sometimes – left to roam along a path they make as they go – left to night and night's lonely sounds mixing with the whir of the processor fan. Cuz left alone long enough a fellow 'll prob'ly wander back the way he came or end up comin' around another way – it doesn't much matter. And, if he's been on the run, he might cut through an open field of a sudden and turn himself in to his pursuers, who won't at all understand his action. They'll handcuff him right there in the middle of the field, sure, but they won't take him straight away to a cruiser – they'll let him sit on a stump or ledge for a while not knowin' why they done it but givin' him some time. That's all I want – I want some time like that – some time to think it out.

❖

What it means is I am not enough...to save you – that there's a million trillion other life-forms out there with the same dream, and sure, when we find each other there'll be some interstellar partyin' for a while – though I wouldn't completely rule out an idiotic extermination – but after that we'll have to get moving again. Because *moving* gives it the illusion of life – what we are, I mean – the expansion of consciousness – space exploration – multiple dimensions – hope. I think there is no more religion – that it's the Holocaust commandment, "Thou shalt not believe in gods." Has superstition perished then? I know I don't get much scared anymore. I'm standing in a vast, empty riverbed: it's gone – the whole thing – sucked away. At least Jennie's here – she's my girl.

❖

I feel like it's gotta end soon, that I can't unfold anymore – not planted in a flower box anyway – so I gotta gingerly dig myself up, carry myself with gardening gloves, and replant me near a stream. Then, after that, I gotta just leave myself alone out there awhile...'n hope I don't get eaten by a goat.

Alright, alright – hold on! Now folks, don't think I've lost sight a' what bein' an Annelid means. Believe me, I'm not crazy about makin' myself out to be a daffodil or daisy, but these 'r all just posies and ploys – really, I'm still a worm at primitive heart, or hearts. Bein' a worm though, listen – it means a life of neglect 'n bein' trod upon. It means findin' yer best friend desiccated. It means wrigglin' nightmares of yellow beaks diving down from the sky. And ask – just ask any halved survivor – they'll tell you: it means giant pink appendages reaching into our topsoil, snatching us up only to tear us, to pierce us upon curved thorns and drown us!

But hey, life ain't all bad. I mean...

No, I can't do it. I just wanna quit. I wanna be done. I don't want to try anymore. If it won't come – or if it'll only come in a thousand fragmented voices – cuz they're not *seg*mented – then I've honestly had enough. And who'll have the patience for so many truncations, so much trying too hard, such exhausting of purpose...?

I wish I could go back – go back and write something just the opposite – something entirely indulgent, whimsical, crude. I wish that were in me t' do, but it isn't. I wish I could turn my prose inside out. I wish I wrote poems, a whole book of poems – real ones, not the stilted makeshift sideways shit leaning up over there against the shed.

I wish I didn't always have to come back to worrying about faith and being alone, conjuring "aw, what's the use of things" and "maybe there's secret gods hiding nearby, watching from behind rocks." Fact is, I can't bear the mantle, it's too much. I must be all growed up.

I have these two dreams. Actually, I haven't had either one in a long time, but for some reason they just popped into my head so I'm gonna tell you about them. In the first I'm at the top of this steep waterslide, straight with dips here and there, that must go down a thousand feet, and I'm scared but I'm also excited, and the ride is exhilarating – wow – I love it. In the other I'm standing at the edge of a canyon way up over a waterfall and the kids around me are jumping hundreds of feet into the pool below the falls, which is very very deep, and I'm terrified and I don't understand why any kid would jump but there are all kinds of 'em swimming away like ants down there after they've done it, maybe even my brother...so why can't I? And these dreams – I don't know which one my life is – or if it's either. I don't even know what I want.

    I should shave and iron – after all, I've got work tomorrow – because that's what I do, I work.

    Let it end.

After the Worm

Today I want to make the paper soft because maybe I am, or my mood, my feather-down attitude. Let's have some pillow talk, or at least let's touch each other's hands.

I want to sit here like a clock, and tick and tick, and tock and tock, and feel the waruhmth of my skin, and somehow, someway, let you in. There's the door, I'll just lie flat, 'n cover the floor like a welcome mat, stretched across from wall to wall, present underneath it all – listening through the boards, breathing through the flue, feeling through the furniture, existent just for you.

❖

Will it strike me? Not a story: will *life* strike me... as a thing sufficiently worthwhile...as meaningful endeavor? Will it carry me over to the side of the living, bodily, upside down, like a canoe at a portage? Will it move me to act, to pose, to postulate – to paddle myself upstream toward the source, to feel myself running hard against the current, launching my bark up over the rocks, getting crazy looks from the salmon?! Will it save me long enough to get back to my spawning ground? Because I want to be a kid again – a young fry – only this time, *one who knows*.

❖

Used to be a poet plopped down on his elbow in an orchard 'n let rip a gorgeous discourse on plants and clouds. Now, there being no *in*spiration left, it's all a fella can do to *ex*spirit a few externals – liven 'em up with pastel curtains or a flounce. Cuz there's no life *in* an object anymore, no pantheistic essence, no benignant forces at work – no Aeolian harps, just wind chimes. What would it take to bring back inspiration? And, if we cannot, shall we christen a new poetic state of mind – call it *resuscitation*...? Vates and scops, condemn me – cast me out of your idyllic garden! Fact is, I don't think I'm much like you anymore so it's probably best I leave. In case you want to know, I'm headin' east.

❖

Out walking last night alone, taking the whole of streets and fields and forest and dirt and sand, taking it all in and concentrating, with hands outstretched, raising my arms slowly from my sides, I tried. But it's like you can't let go your orbit. The rules of sense-making are old rules...older than π – just as stale.

❖

What is it we really do here anyway besides just try to get by? There are all these made-up careers and hobbies and frittering interests and avocations but no raison d'être anywhere in the plotline...though I suppose if there was one there could be only one. But ah: multiplicity! – Quadruple duple helical plots and subplots twisting tautly together like bridge cables, or fatly, like sea-soaked hawsers. Still...are they not, with all those twines though, *one* strand, whether they mean or not? Am I not lost in – loose with – so much fiber?!

Is any purpose subjoined to our dexterity? – Any reason to grab at inertia in a welter so profoundly deep, so fast, so unyielding? No Medevac copter hovers over the existential flood to drop a cord to the drowning... unless *that's* the skein that life is – *that's* the rope that saves us. Does it end with hauling me out?!

❖

Tired of playing the petty banker – 'd like to try a new role, say, troubadour – or something lacking refinement – longshoreman, perhaps. And if all *those* jobs are taken, how 'bout just bein' a hobo for a while, or maybe a mail-order bride, or a seamstress, or a little boy in a coal mine, or parts for new people? Okay then, fuck it, let's switch – little boy, you come on over here 'n fund these loans, I'll take your grimy pick. Best of luck to yah! [Slaps boy on the back. Boy coughs.] Seriously, though – remember when boys was chimney sweeps? Yup – that was way back. Nowadays they get to make sneakers maybe. Golly, I'm wicked. Wicked enough to write? I think so! Feels good not to care. Yes – yes it does.

❖

If I'm vowing to write every day at lunch then not all can be for show – some must just follow, like digestion does my sandwich and fruit. So I shall sit here awhile and let myself settle. Calm and repose. And I shall sip at my coffee: "sip." And I shall look around this barren room, full of empty chairs, easels and dry-erase boards, and not find one good reason why any of it should endure. Or why I should, or thinking. No where

I go and no one I meet can last. Everything falls away. Nothing remains – not even a page.

❖

The sobering *how*...of finding aliment. Letting yourself be gulled by a quack. Bird talk.

❖

Call it a free-write but believe me, it developed... didn't start from nothin' merely...was there – there the whole time – was cookin' – roastin' – steamin' away like baked beans buried in one o' them big pots...uh, whaddya call 'em...oh, I'll look it up later. Dug up them beans though and dug up the coals...or Coles – just one (wonder what *that* means) – then made a circle of stones – a fire ring – all the way 'round that hole, that empty beanless hole. Matter of fact, I made a figure 8 – no, that's a lie – but I made it pretty for the rites, the hopelessly supererogatory rites every invocation o' which freezes the fires of hope. Okay, that's too much – that's bombast maybe – hyperbole. Well, so what if it is! The pit, the legume-lacking pit I undug in the woods – *that's* what I'm talkin' about, 'n how the beans taste. Ah, but who cares, this 's got nowhere to go. Movin' on then, to brussels sprouts. Oh, and "crock" – the word was "crock."

Right in the middle, the center of my head, is a hole or recess th't everythin' is tryin' to grow around – it's a pitfall in the jungle, but all that's at the bottom is bones, old bones – like nothin's been caught in that hole for years. God, I hope it's only growin' over 'n not gettin' filled in – unless it's supposed to – unless it's with fragrant beans.

❖

Yeah, I keep things, I keep things from Jennie... from Reed – hell, I even keep things from my clavicle – but does that make me closed or cagey? I can be private with my thoughts is all, especially the ones I'm not sure about. What's just mine then? What's my inmost solace? My inmost fear? HOPE – and DESPAIR – with hardly a sliver of luncheon meat between, though certainly plenty of cheese.

❖

The question does not seem to arise on Fridays – Fridays are all euphoria. Fridays seem to encapsulate the hope one has, the solitude-of-a-channel-swimmer's hope perhaps, but some part of real hope anyway. Friday today, I mean – this Friday – this week's Friday.

❖

Was out in the garage one afternoon sweeping and picking up when the broom fell out of my hand – unremarkable, I know, but when it hit the concrete made a hollow sound. I looked closely at the floor there and noticed a crack that seemed oddly straight, and then another running parallel a couple of feet away. After running my fingers along them I realized they weren't cracks at all but grooves. Soon I'd traced the outline of a more or less perfect square in the concrete surface. How did I not notice this before? I grabbed a couple of screwdrivers from a toolbox and worked them underneath. Pretty soon I was able to free the block just enough to wedge a crowbar under, then I pried it up and heaved it away. Looking into the hole I saw, a few feet below, a dusty staircase leading down into the dark.

I lowered myself onto a small landing at the top of the stairs. From there I could see, at the very bottom, what looked to be the rooms of my own house palely lit. I edged down the staircase into the rooms, and now they seemed one large, vaguely enclosed space, indistinctly dimensioned, and sharing the interior features of several houses I'd lived in throughout my life. Around me were many objects out of my past. From a window nearby I saw my dad in a driveway conversing with a stranger – he looked like he did when I was eight or ten. My mom's knitting lay out next to a rocking chair that was still faintly rocking. There were shadowy paintings, obscurely figured rugs, even odors that seemed somehow familiar – and a brooding quietness. All of it felt deeply mysterious and significant.

Throughout the entire experience – try as I might to understand what it meant – I was afflicted by a strange anxiety that became increasingly more intense until finally I was forced to leave. When I'd climbed up to the garage again I immediately pulled the concrete block back over the hole, then I just slumped against a wall for a while, exhausted. The thought of the place consumed me for days but my anxiety remained extreme, almost debilitating. Finally, after resealing the floor and smoothing it over, I started to feel better. And then something occurred to me: if I have a secret door or portal or whatever it is under my house then maybe other people do too.

So I go to my friend's house and bring him over, not explaining why really cuz I'm afraid he won't believe me. I chisel out where I'd just resealed the floor, show him the staircase, and send him down for a look – before long though the anxiety's back and it's worse than ever so I shout for him to come up out of there and I seal the hole again. This time it takes weeks for my nerves to recover.

While I'm recuperating, come to find out my friend's been jackhammering all through his garage but he's found nothing – apparently he's become obsessed with the idea of this thing. A few days later, after breaking the jackhammer, when he's just about lost his wits and he's down in his basement taking a pickaxe to the foundation, way over in a corner he finds a tunnel. He sounds almost manic on the phone telling me this, which is very worrisome, but I've got to see what's there so I hurry over. At the end of the tunnel there's this hatch sort of like the block in my garage but it seems like it's been there a lot longer. With incredible effort we're able to lift it out of the way. He shines a flashlight down – there's a staircase alright, but with human remains on it, like someone was trapped down there and couldn't get out.

My friend is never the same after that. We push the block back into place and fill the tunnel with dirt and debris. He pays to get his basement and garage fixed. He tries to take things up again like before but he can't. Gradually he loses his hold on life.

❖

>Slipping over the abyss, crab-like –
>Clutching back with cumbersome claw
>Through the settling cloud of twitched up sand –
>Clutching back at nothing – not water nor air –
>Down, over you go, out of ken, out of care.

2004

The lights in this room become me,
The chairs, this corner of a meeting table,
These cords and plugs and strike plates.
I am them and they are me –
We are one room together,
One quiet, tidy, climate-controlled boardroom
Hurtling through space and time,
Or so they say.

❖

What do you want to do? Whatever it is, stay in the game – life don't stop cuz you blew out your knee. Maybe lying there on the turf, writhing, looking up at the sky, is too much living. Too much means go 'til it's not enough! Too much means get a shot of cortisone – bite the bullet – heal thyself – *choose* thy cliché – but *get up* – hobbling if you have to – and head figuratively back to the huddle.

❖

"Huh – somehow I thought there'd be more." That's the phrase I think, or close enough. It's from a book or story I read recently – can't remember quite where I read it. Anyhow, supposedly it sums up the journey from childhood to adulthood and the attendant feeling of disappointment – to wit, our expectations diminish as the world around us shrinks into something nearer and therefore more familiar, lacking mystery. You know how when you visit your middle school or kindergarten years later it seems so much smaller, even the house you grew up in? Well, it's not that it's smaller – or even that you've grown up – but that you can take it all in now, your comprehension can account for the distribution of classrooms and pupils' resources, the school bus schedule, and all the other machinery that makes school *work*. Damn how it fits and makes sense! Used to be you assumed it fit cuz there was too much you didn't understand besides – arithmetic, for instance – and that *a priori* faith is the magic stuff of childhood memories, like an ethereal glue really, binding fast and holding true through all but the most confounding upheavals. Sooner or later though, the glue starts to run out or wear away or just not work anymore on new experiences...and so we humbly take to grout.

I'm starting a new paragraph so that folks don't lose me on this, but we're still talking about the glue. Now, assuming my theory holds, this glue is only good for kids, and glue-sniffing the past is all nostalgic adults can do to bring back the feeling, the flow. Did we "think there'd be more" when we grew up because we thought the glue 'd keep working, keep filling in the seams ahead of us with possibility? I mean, that's all we knew, right?! It must be.

So why do I want to write, cuz I know it's not to get back to the glue like it is for some people? I've singed a nostril hair or two with the sniffing and really, that's enough for me. I'm tired of sniffing glue – tired of running around and jumping over the Lawn Sprinklers of the Past. I'm almost forty now and if I keep huffing and hurdling sprinklers somebody's gonna call the cops... and you know what, they'll be doing me a favor.

So next idée fixe – one from a few years back but

still in my head waiting to be parsed. Yeah, I'm talkin' about omnipotence, the omnipotent newborn. See, the way I figure, there's this crazy confusedness when you're born – just a jumble of lights and air and unmuffled voices and trying to breathe. Besieged from the outset of *ex utero vita* there nevertheless persists, for a time, a pre-natal trust in the purity of undifferentiated experience – aka, caps please, The Union with the Mother. Well anyway, that monistic oneness or union inherently *makes sense* – empowers in a very basic way – so it's only with profound reluctance and intense frustration – kicking and screaming, as it were – that a child's compelled to give it up, to move away from the comfort and sanctity of that feeling toward individuation – rather like a super tot being gradually drained of their powers.

Now this is the one I think I'm stuck on – this is the illusion I can't shake off – I even have flying dreams every now and then that try to bring me back.

Or maybe it's *not* the Oneness thingy or the magic glue – maybe it's something else. Maybe I'm stuck on a grandiosity & depression carousel and some other bastard's already grabbed the ring so I'll be bobbin' up and down on a faggy plastic pony 'til the end of time. *Un*merrily, one way or another, most all of us are caught up in going around something, whether we much know it or not.

Suppose I remind myself yet again not to measure people against those silly ideal versions of selves none of us can ever live up to. Suppose I make mine a doppelganger to boot, so that maybe I'll dream about a sinister little anti-Tris and thereby teach myself a thing or two...instead of falling asleep in a stuffy third floor front bedroom with rickety single pane windows and a light fixture hole patched over only to wake up in dreamland flying around saving comely young lasses and generally trying to impress people.

Bah, it's no good – I'm not exactly riding a carousel but there's a pattern for sure – I just dangle my privates out here and there to recoup a little of the shame I've inflicted, then save the document in the proper folder and call it a day. Heck, I can almost make out my bony backside ahead – in the mists on the horizon – dick hangin' low, flappin' in tomorrow's breeze.

❖

Jennie says I gotta write even if I'm tired or just uninspired – write every night for twenty minutes at least. What about? I haven't a thought t' put to paper this evening and still I'm mandated twenty minutes. I'll give you twenty middle fingers for your twenty goddamn minutes! And anyway, who has the right to mandate anything of me – I'm not the tobacco industry, I'm a human being. Mandate this woman:

Took a three flush dump earlier – now that's an impressive number – a small number, yes, I grant you, but given the context, a number to respect. Five is the record. I was telling Jennie, "Imagine a five flusher – that's just something you don't hear about often – and I'm not talking about a plunger-assisted fiver, no sirree! – I'm talking five bursting basins of..."

Really – that was starting to get a little self-indulgent – and it's not like I'm obsessed with fecal matter(s), it's just that keeping on for twenty minutes ain't easy and if cheap gross-outs 'll get me there sooner, I'm gonna go for it.

But let's talk about something else, huh. Let's talk about highway infrastructure and who's gonna pay for that shit cuz I can tell you right now it sure 's hell ain't gonna be me – I'll take the bus for fuck sake. And you *know* all them contracts are going to the uh...that friggin' union...uh – Teamsters – the friggin' Teamsters – and they're a bunch a' thugs you gotta bribe anyhow cuz they work for the mob. Or they are *in* the mob – I get confused – anyhow, point is, they are real sonuvabitches and don't cross 'em or you'll end up like whatsizname that Hoffa guy Nicholson played in the movie that time with...uh...Tom Cruise. Oh yeah: *You Can't Handle the Truth* – I think that's what it was called. Whatever. Like I care – I'm just trying to blow twenty minutes – think I got five left...four...

Shouldn't have said anything...now I'm stuck... Well look, I could at least end this respectably, restore some sense, and put the blue collar rant to rest until I really need it – 'til I'm in a pinch – 'til I unwittingly stumble into the middle of a Hells Angels rally, or find my name on a welfare roll sandwiched between a couple of Micks.

❖

About halfway through my long walk tonight I stopped, sat down on a bench, and decided that 2004 is a lost year for me – or that mid 2003 to mid 2004 is...or was. I'm not even sure how I determined this, or if I decided on anything else in particular, other than *moving forward*, cuz as it is I'm moving laterally, not exactly sidling the year but not stepping off the curb of it either. Anyhow, if I did there'd probably be a big splashy puddle in my very first step that'd make me feel like "what's the use."

Didn't think about *the* or *a* story – didn't think about life as "continual allegory"[17] – thought instead about pulling down this sequiny star in front of me like it was a window shade and pleading with it, "Help me out here, will yah?!" The thing kept twinkling away though and the bench was getting hard, so I got up and kept going.

Not long afterward I passed this strange guy who then caught up and overtook me a few minutes later. And he'd stop short from time to time or stagger a little and motion like he was swinging a baseball bat...and I think maybe he wanted me to know that he was a homosexual who liked sports because maybe it looked like I was one who liked sports too (in fairness, I was wearing some cool jersey shorts a friend gave me). Well, I made my trudge a little more pronounced and dipped my head even further than usual and that all seemed finally to convince the guy I wasn't the piece of ass he was looking for cuz he stopped swinging, sped up, and disappeared ahead. Now, of course, a lot of that's surmise – I mean, he might've had some kind of baseball-bat-swing tic type thing he couldn't shake cuz he'd run out of meds.

Not *wild* surmise though.[18] No. God forbid. Wouldn't want any literary seepage to congeal around my casual walk. And really, that's the sort of walk it was – I didn't bother to work over any story ideas, I just kept going. I was walking out my creative energies, letting loose the year through my feet, expending the thing, crushing it into a crappy vintage.

❖

On my walk tonight decided I'd better take some chances so I went up past the homeless shelter, bearing witness to much colorful language and pent-up rage, loitering, close talking at windows, and sleeping across sidewalks. The debris of hard living was everywhere around me and I kicked it provokingly...but I wasn't mugged or propositioned or followed this time (that I know of), and one guy even muttered in acknowledgement when our eyes met, which stirred my patrician sympathies acutely. Did I learn a damn thing about fear though? No. I probably just relearned – confirmed – that I'm a goddamn snob – that I'm afraid of real people and real problems and have no intention of volunteering in my community any time soon.

❖

There's nothing compelling me to write at all but the cat is warm on my lap and I am disinclined therefore to move. Besides, I'm sitting here with the damn program open anyway – was writing notes for tomorrow's meeting. And now I've nothing more to say – "Breathe, breathe in the air..."[19] No really, nothing. We may have another roommate in a couple of weeks. Oh, and I may need some sort of writing lesson six years from now when the urge comes back. Gave a hundred bucks to the Red Cross. No, I didn't give any blood – would consider it though. Balls are sweaty. I really should erase that but in a hundred years no one's balls 'll sweat anymore because of high-tech underwear so it's important somebody document the phenomenon before it's gone like the Old Man of the Mountain.[20] Ball sweat makes a good segue into the subject of process – into my desperate 'no holds barred' style of keep-on-writing-no-matter-what-you-have-to-say-just-don't-stop. And ball sweat is universal, like love, and cavities, and the universe...at least among guys...non-eunuchs. Haven't I talked about eunuchs pretty recently? I feel like I have. Well, they'll still be around after that underwear comes out – hell, specialty shops 'll still carry the old model just for them. Eunuchs – what are they thinking choppin' their nuts off anyway? Remember when there used to be bear-baiting? Well, are there any contemporary descriptions of that? Or of trips to the Oracle at Delphi? Quaggas? I like thoughts that are loosely associated – so do demented old people and hippy psychoanalysts, non-eunuchs who probably don't even experience ball sweat. Bastards.

❖

I know, I already covered this on the way home from work with Jennie, but I think it bears repeating, even if only as an admonition about my character – about character – about me being – everyone – a lot of us anyway – too disappointingly human too damned often.

So yesterday I get home and I've got like half an hour to get ready for tennis when I remember that it's Tuesday – Grandfather got out of the hospital *this morning* – so I probably oughtta give him a call. Now I don't know just what the proportion of obligatory to genuine, heartfelt concern was in me at that moment, but the quantities of neither were generous. So I call the house and my uncle answers. I ask him about Grandfather, who's obviously nearby, and say something like, "Oh, uh, he's alright?...Cuz I don't know if I have time to talk to him – I'm on my way out the door to play tennis." Then I realize that maybe I should talk to him anyway. After my uncle gets him on the phone I find out he's only really home because legions of doctors have collectively thrown themselves on their sterilized swords in despair at the multiplying complications his health has assumed so, you know, maybe I shouldn't 've been going on about how I've gotta go play some stupid game when this man – my *grandfather* – is debating whether to have his kidneys drained three times a week or just pack it in. Nice going, real nice. I smooth it out as best I can with a few extra well-placed solicitations but the effort just feels more and more self-conscious and mechanical...which, of course, makes bothering at all seem like a charade.

Well, somehow or other the conversation finally ends and now I definitely feel like an insensitive jerk – one with only fifteen minutes to eat and get moving – but yeah, a jerk. So I turn on the TV and start to get ready, putting sneakers on, getting my tennis bag in order, doing a stretch or two, throwing down a micro-waveable. The news is on and in my mind I'm sort of backing out the late charges and penalties accrued for the botched phone call when they go to this story about a guy who's visiting the scene of a horrific accident he'd been in when he was like two. Here's the thing: he's got no face. What I mean is his ears are *he has none* and his nose *isn't there* and even most of his lips are gone – apparently, the car he'd been in had caught fire and he was strapped in his safety seat so he couldn't move. And this is one of the kindest, most pleasant and good-natured guys you could ever meet – he even says "he wouldn't change a thing" about his life. So who the hell am I? I'm watching this man beam – I mean, if sunlight could come out of a dude it would come out of him – and I wouldn't want to look like that but still, how incredibly fortunate he is to have been so much loved! How important and how necessary it is. I am missing something – something he has. It's really simple actually: he's got no face but he knows who he is and what he wants, why he does things or doesn't, and that nothing has to turn out in any particular way. He's who I want to be.

❦

It's pretty staggering to think how little I have to hold on to. Or that I hold it at all. There's *life* and, trust me, it's got some tensile strength – the rest though, ideas and whatnot – the rest holds about like rope stranded with cotton candy.

❖

Who am I in relation to the dust whence I came? All the intelligence I've got, all the strength, cannot draw me back one dram closer to the beginning, the divergence. Or to the end when we're all poured back in again to the fresh water butt stored deep in the hold of a mystery caravel voyaging o'er the limitless seas of the sky.

Goddamn limits. Goddamn barrel. Gimme a dram 'o *mean* to get over this sea *sickness*! Let me up on the fucking deck! Why do you hold us back?! Better to perish in flames!

❖

I swear – I swear up 'til now just about every-damn-body's been living in a fog, and now that it's blown off here and there, a few of us see that there's nothing beyond, or that the prospect of discovering hopeful signs is dim. Of course, the truth is most of us like a good fog, and are equipped with portable fog machines should the weather clear.

❖

Now...**when I eat turkey** I get a piece of white meat on the fork, I stick it in the mashed potatoes, then I dab it with stuffing – sort of a three pronged attack. I keep doing that for a while then I switch over to the peas, maybe mixed with a little stuffing or squash because you know how those darn peas get everywhere. After that I go back to the turkey for a while, sip the Chardonnay, and break for a roll – it's like a little dessert midway through...so long as it's moist – it's gotta be moist. Then it's turkey again, seconds, and another moisty – grab that second one early if you have to!

And while you're eating here are a few tips. Number one: *your chief competition will always come from siblings* – you are a perceived threat no matter the locale so make sure that, having ascertained the direction of the flow of food, you situate yourself so as to receive before brother and sis. Second tip: *do not underestimate grandma* – she won't eat much but she will get preference as the tastier dishes run out – encourage her to extra helpings of turnip and beets before the dark meat starts to peek through the white. Third: *don't get caught looking ahead* – nobody really cares about the damn pies (they never taste that good anyway) but people start talking about them with exaggerated conviviality when there's still plenty of turkey left to be eaten...and then it don't get ate! And last: *emphasize fullness proactively* – that way you'll be "too stuffed" to make good on that of-course-I'll-try-aunt's-rutabaga promise made earlier in the meal.

❖

One of them damn Trojan viruses trying to infect my computer so I guess I'll doodle for a while 'til Norton Utilities ferrets it out. Okay, so maybe I was being bad, peeling back a little the wallpaper behind the fridge just to see what grime lay beneath. I got a black market side too, though you wouldn't know cuz I keep it hid... which is not to say I would've died from syphilis by now if these were Victorian times, but I mighta made an ill-advised proposition or two. I wonder that I haven't yet compromised my health – but for other reasons – the very same which provoke these unseemly remarks.

No, I'm not gonna say "cheerleaders" or "pregnant chicks" are my internet vices, or even something more outré. Let's just gloze the kinky stuff anyhow – presume a pituitary's worth of iniquity – since the real subject here is not exhibitionism of one sort or another but morbid introspection...and, sooner or later, the upshot *desperation of means*.

Cuz I just want to get through it, lawlessly or by the books, prudently or pruriently, but through to an achieved maturity, of voice and manner – through to clarity and synthesis and simplicity with no extraneous crap. No wait, I'd like some extraneous crap, I changed my mind – or do I mean extra, superfluous matter, whether it's crap or not? Indeed, what *do* I mean?! Briefly, I mean to get through, and I'll do a little time in solitary if I have to – hence *desperation of means*.

But that's disingenuous. It all is. I talk about rape and murder because I cannot move from my chair. I have werewolf and vampire dreams because I'm haunted by an undead passion. And I don't move and can't wake up because...because I've lost the inclination? Because nothing moves me? A revolution might – or an earthquake – or really being a werewolf or vampire.

This world holds you close. It's all you can do to get some distance between your breath and the glass fogging up in front. All you can do to rip off a few successful metaphors that go some ways – further than you do – toward conveying the distance between flesh and other. And what the deuce is *other*? And why can't it yield a little?! – Give us a hint now and then, a shadow on a wall, a taste, a sound, a keyhole to peep through – preferably into a boudoir...

Truthfully, it hurts to move. It hurts to even think about moving, and I think about it all the time. I'm obsessed with getting up off my ass and doing any damn thing, and thinking about doing it and not doing it sickens and twists. Lust is thought inaction.[21] Desperation of Means.

2005

I was watching a PBS show about Shakespeare and now I'm thinking about writing – the urge...to write or not to write – whether it's in me – whether I'm only sucked dry of creativity by work-time expenditures – whether the urge, the impulse to write may merely lie dormant, waiting for me to quit my damn job or transfer back in town to a position with fewer responsibilities, so I can resume taking lunch breaks at the bagel place and walks in and around Monument Square. Or maybe – what I'm really hoping – maybe *it* will let me know – or *I'll* know when *it's* coming back, if it is, and a decision will finally be made – or at least I'll tease myself with the idea of one, a *final* decision, even though there's never likely to be any decisive break, just a meandering sidewalk crack.

What does Shakespeare tell me? He tells me that I need a shot of joie de vivre, that I haven't lived, and that I don't take enough risks and should therefore expose myself to a Petri dish of plague on the nonce. Truthfully though, he also tells me that I should wait a little longer too, just to be sure, before I quit my damn job to hawk quartos in the Square.

❧

Thinking about my grandfather, who turned 81 today, and who likely won't turn 82, or 81 ½. About the impulse to write again, and why it may take a day like today, rife with indignity, to bring it back...or sensibly less – a well-timed warble perhaps, or particle of sand glinting just so on the pavement. About how I don't even know why it's here today rather than on some other when Grandfather was dying, and whether it insults him – and diminishes me – to make a spiritual out of this unseasonable summer flurry. About that rope he's got hanging from a crossbeam, or the commode he swings to with one dead leg and one living. About the *living* room hardly changed after twenty-five years despite the electric hospital bed and the toilet right there in the middle. About sitting in the backseat of my brother's car coming home, clutching the plastic handle above the window and leaning on my arm just as Grandfather leans on his when he clutches that rope, only not with my head drooping forward, not with my whole side shaking. About the couth or uncouth in recording such comparisons. About being 32 but not knowing how to or if I sufficiently honor him – turning it all toward me, as though I were the subject not him...or it. Or her: Grandma has to go to the hospital tomorrow for another biopsy – she didn't want to talk about that though because it was his birthday.

❖

>Margins of highway and surging sea,
>Of ragweed, bane, and yarrow
>Form the outlines of my inner life.
>It's kind of sad really – I mean,
>I can get much farther in my car
>Than I can in my mind.
>
>So much the working hours now drain me
>I feel fenced off from greenery
>From the risk even of a single leafy rumination –

I'm a toy cherry in a park
Too small for promenades.

And the ocean – the broad flat limitless
Expanse of ocean – is one more chimera,
One more snapping yellow caution line
Not to be got beyond.

And the groaning highway, late at night,
Haunts my thoughts
Like the ghost of some explorer
Whose life was no doubt briefer
But didn't suffer borders.

❖

Gloom is a morning red
The color in my head
And languid pools of crimson
Gather next the bed.

Invisible are gouts like these
Portentous of disease
But present nonetheless
Having leached right out of me.

❖

 Empty and without subject – indeed, wishing there was one – a trope, a motif, an overarching theme instead of...scattered leaves.
 Have I fashioned myself a place – a situation – outside of risk – is that what salary and status entitle one to?
 Just now a blue jay tromping through the branches of a maple outside, yanking blossoms off senselessly and

clicking with ecstatic glee, totally immersed in self – and how else other could he be?!

❖

Was the earth branched out at one end
Or some spiry peak connected to the moon
Then all of Nature's seeming would bear
One mystical relation, and the rules,
Somehow changed – different than they are –
Would twist and spin and swirl together
In an immense, yet elegant, kaleidoscope –
And it would turn and turn and turn and turn
And there'd be no pain in its easing.

❖

I see with eye-popping clarity
How simple my world is
And therefore, what a farce.
I feel insufferably
How much more there must be
That I, lowly being, cannot see,
But that possibly,
By some chance synergy
Of thinking, through poetry,
Might bring me
Into a new place
Where gods exist again.

❖

(After two weeks in Italy)

Having swallowed the vomit of my weltschmerz, am now moving toward a more meaningful cosmos...No, not really, but keeping the example of Florentine majesty before me, hope is I'll dump my job and write – looking to transfer within the bank at the very least. Meanwhile, it's become downright wintry here, and only being civilized keeps me from seeking out a cave.

Sooth, la! – Not a hint of meaning in the flight of birds or close examination of guts. – Haruspection? I dunno, something like that. So – no hope here of any guidance... unless we're counting windsocks. Michelangelo – Supergenius – even he believed in the Christian god. What half-decent writer ever came along who believed in, not nothing at all (plenty of middling scribblers there), but that they'd never get even the least understanding of the not-nothing-but-still-not-much-more-either-sorry? Indeed.

❖

This morning is all blue echo, echoing blue. And the sky is reverberant with machine noise, so that people do not seem present, only shadowy remnants of their having been. I imagine a world that is all machines, snorting cacophonously into the cloudless azure. And there is no one questioning what powers their engines, fuels their discord. Like dinosaurs they continue on uninterruptedly for eon after eon until one day, far distant, the lack of routine maintenance catches up with them: sparkplugs start to go, gaskets fail, cylinder pumping stalls and coughs to a stop...and then there is stillness, just as there'd been if we were here and gone extinct, only without the panic and brooding.

❖

Excitement in a mood, in a feeling merely, expectant of some good, on a Saturday. Excitement in seeing so much squalor and muck, sand and dust, so inexhaustibly pile up, ready. Excitement in listening to a Saturday workman, and Saturday traffic and toiling – in sliding by all the troubles of landlords and bus drivers and beepered call-ins – in recognizing that my place requires not a finger raised nor card punched – that I may sit here and scribble alllll day if I like. I won't, of course, but the peace of mind granted 'll persist for a while and make my time fully less anguished than, say, a Monday evening, giving me the space and breadth to contemplate *yellow leaves on porphyry* – a few green ones left on the trees – raw chilly noses and boots coming out – or the harsh autumn light with its gloomily precise delineations of shadows on grass and streets.

    Ah, I wish I begged of definition like the seasons – not that a million portraitists easeled up to my door, but... or *no* – that I *did* not – that I could get around the whole of me, like I did the Coliseum, and see into the middle like it was some glass paperweight with old buttons glazed in – *not* that I so much defined as with dictionary or slide rule, but that I could polish up the glass and turn myself to best address, most becoming attitude. Now I place me back down on the table, draw a curtain to let in the October light...and just walk away.

2006

This morning around 4am a lone thunderclap, loud as I've ever heard, and simultaneous with the lightning. I awoke thinking, "What if this is the end?", though I knew how extremely unlikely that was – still, the thought was there, provisionally, waiting for a blast wave to corroborate, or the continuance of traffic to disconfirm. Is that how it ended in Hiroshima? Were there people outside the vaporization zone that heard what I heard last night...waited...then had their roofs and skin shorn off as they lay in bed? – Everyday people just looking at the ceiling, wondering if a meteor had hit perhaps, even chuckling a little at the ridiculousness of the notion, then whisked away...or flayed alive by the searing winds, however you want to look at it.

❖

What was it Proust wrote about so goddamn endlessly – or how 'bout Balzac – hell, James even? How is it they had so much to say? The current runs thin in me – it's a creek – a rivulet. I think there's a pretty high content of ore in the sediment, but still, what's it matter when the waterway under discussion amounts to a trickle?!

❖

Just looking for a subject as far removed from death and depression and despair and longing and Dis as possible...though there's no escaping the blankness of succession in an endeavor like *this* – to wit, filling an endless page – one that goes on forever – that succeeds always, reflexively, automatically, relentlessly, to another empty, white and staring sheet without blemish or watermark or crease or dog-ear or smell or edge or sibilance. It's all electronical these days, and not a dang thing you can do but say "huh," and try to fill it up again.

...It's all nonsense besides – *this* stuff – *writing*. The real stuff of living is preverbal postverbal antiverbal *not* verbal anyway, and it'd be totem-raising to entertain a more exalted notion or idea of what language can do or capacitate. Believe me, it ain't that much – it can limn out plans pretty well – draw borders with a degree of fineness – but coloring the flesh – getting the chest to rise and fall with each successive breath – impossible – and to attempt the effect can only lead to ludicrous results, like Shakespeare's soliloquies...the which, admittedly, may also comprise our most valiant assays. Well, I say give over the attempt – don't bother trying to articulate emotions. Forget it – just quit – fake an injury – take your signing bonus and buy a beach house in Bermuda – retire in style – that's what I'm gonna do...just give me time. Art shmart.

❖

I'm at a train terminal – must've gone the wrong way when I disembarked – somehow I'm caught in the line for a chain restaurant. I climb the faux pergola to get a better view – looks like it's gonna be a long wait. I'm supposed to be meeting friends at a movie theater on the other end of the terminal so I make a shallow dive out over the queue and glide to the far side, then walk briskly toward a bank of steel-framed glass doors separating the food court from the flanking corridors – the theater entrance is just on the other side. Where are my friends (vaguely, some old college buddies)? Then I see them entering through the same doors but they don't look at all pleased to see me – one or two mutter comments indicating the collective opinion, of disapproval perhaps, resentment. Apparently they'd seen me flying and now feel differently about me, even suggest that I watch some other film, before abruptly walking off as a group.

The place – this concourse – it's bustling with travelers and commuters going every which way, looking in boutique windows, scanning the marquee, hurrying in and out of the doors – and I'm getting angry, incredibly, viciously angry. I turn and storm straight ahead through an opening in the crowd and launch myself upward. There's a skylight directly above so, lest I injure people with the raining shards, I blast through the ceiling instead – first tiles, then vents and pipes and tar paper, all in a phenomenally destructive instant – and now I'm streaking through the sky, twisting and screaming with rage. And I fly that way for a few minutes maybe, 'til I'm calm again, then I start to descend. I pick out a quiet alleyway...and then just change my mind – fuck it, what do I care – so I land midstride on a busy sidewalk and simply start walking, I don't know where. Somebody sees me – a woman, naturally, beautiful and confident. She approaches – or no, just says something from the other side of the street...and next thing you know we're making out at her place in the shower only we're both still dressed I think and soap is starting to get in my eyes...

❖

Why's this have to be it? Couldn't just a little speck – a smidgeon – of somewhere *else* make it here on a meteor, get analyzed by scientists, tour the world's museums, give us some fucking hope?! I'm not asking for dark matter to light up all at once, or superstrings to unroll like balls of yarn chased by Schrödinger's cat[22] – just a taste, will yah, a single morsel, a fucking crumb from the divine repast – proof that it *happened* is all – proof that something besides a cheap explosion led to the wheel and microwave ovens...– not that I'm tired of zapping pizzas or ziti – don't misunderstand – cooking is a pain in the ass.

❖

You know, rather than stripping away layer after layer in a vain attempt to reach the (chewy?) center perhaps I should add something on – spruce myself up a bit with a few ornaments or embellishments – a coat of varnish – or maybe just papier-mâché. Mom and I made that globe for my science project, remember? We worked damn hard on it. What a pasty mess! – Got the continents on there perfectly though with fine layers of orange tissue paper. Then I'm walking the hallways at the Science Fair and see some other girl's gone and done one twice as nice – hers 's even got felt continents and Velcro so she can show Pangaea and all the shifting and unmerging super-continents. I was a little jealous but I knew we'd worked our butts off and done the best we could. Oh well – got an honorable mention anyway – she came in second, I think – like it matters. So yeah, papier-mâché – gotta smear some on my torso I guess.

❖

Jennie says I really don't take risks – so what kind of risks should I take? I'd like to try acting someday. Scuba diving – is that a risk? What about...uh...visiting poor places – Mexico, maybe? Other people risk themselves unwittingly all the time: ordering Chinese food, skipping exercise, not double-checking to make sure the door's locked. I don't take those risks, at least – I take reasonable chances to secure modest rewards is all – if *they* wanna buy the cheapest batteries for *their* smoke detectors who am I to stop 'em?! So I don't want to run with the bulls or climb the leaning tower of Pisa or spy on North Korea – I have rights too! Just no scrotum.

❖

When'll it end? When'll the "shadow of some unseen power" rise from my limbic system to, uh, shade this dreadful malaise?[23] When'll the sun eclipse without the moon? We're all waiting for the same damn thing – to feel we have a purpose.

Or no – only the depressed people – the other ones, it doesn't even cross their minds. Is that right though? I don't know – *something* doesn't cross their minds – some piece of metaphorical farm equipment – a rototiller maybe. Or could it be they just don't have the *furrow* that gives the bulk of us that plodding and pathetic yet also curiously *rural* look? What the hell am I talking about here, unibrows?! Jesus man, get serious, Christmas is practically tomorrow!

That's all I've got though: levity. I can't be serious about anything – I hide and I hide behind it cuz I'm afraid to look *behind the behind* for fear of the mortal crick it'll give my neck. But I gotta look anyway, no matter what – I gotta try to peel back the skin or sod or I don't know *veneer* from the cheap fucking sideboard of life! I gotta open the drawers and look! I mean, maybe somebody hid money in there!

Pathetic – I can't stop – or I can but it'll crumble into nothing into less than nothing moldery fucking thousandth of a crumb of nothing with no self-expression and no way to get it started so I keep pulling the cord to simulate its starting like an old lawnmower you just won't give up on, that you're 99% sure ain't ever gonna start again but you give it another pull anyways cuz who knows and it makes that *put-put-put* sound so you think for a second "it's gonna start" and it still doesn't but it made that sound so you stand there giving your arm a rest and look around the garage at all the half-finished projects and rusty tools hangin' up and notice a ding or two you hadn't before on the rear quarter panel of your minivan...then you reach back down and yank that ridiculous cord again and wouldn't choices be a fuckload lot simpler if either the engine started up or just didn't turn over at all?! But that ain't life – oh no – and that's why it's such a goddamn miracle. UUUHHHHHH!!... *put-put-put*. Fuck it, one more time – I'll try my left hand.

❖

No righting myself – or conversely, it's like I'm a kayaker who *wants* to flip but can't...like there's this stream I found that goes under a dirt road and into the underworld but you gotta flip over to get there cuz it's a magic culvert that opens upside down and that's the only way you can fit in it anyhow – follow me? Then all of a sudden you come out on the other side and you're there! Way way above you is the earthen ceiling – or wait – is that below...? And thick vines hang from the bottom almost all the way to the top! It takes your brain awhile to get used to this being upside down and you feel like the blood is rushing to your head but you want to explore the place cuz you know you probably won't be able to come back...if you can even *go back* – so you walk a ways out into the jungle with water dripping everywhere and bathtub-size sinkholes and half submerged plants. You climb a ridge to get a little lower down but you still can't see through the vegetation and now you're really getting dizzy so you scramble back to your kayak and paddle out the way you came, fighting as hard as you can against the current, afraid you won't make enough headway to reach the cave you emerged from but then you do get just inside and suddenly your choking on water and upside down for sure and you panic for a second but get yourself righted and discover you're back in the pool near that culvert again, on Wood Road in Gorham, Maine, struggling to catch your breath. A pickup truck barrels past overhead.

❖

I'm in the woods of an animal park at dusk with a couple of rangers who are checking on the condition of the lion enclosure which looks like it's gonna collapse very soon – tonight perhaps – then we walk back up the darkening trail slowly toward the entrance.

❖

Complaints – and on and on and on – is this gonna be my legacy? – Not charity or acts of kindness and maybe a few modest *works* but this: endlessly grousing and carping and poisonous tree frogging my way around and around and then into the black hole of oblivion, only to be emitted – expectorated – like some obscure particle I don't give a damn about. I deploy all the learning and pop knowledge and multiple meanings and allusions I can muster – I pile on the freight then move toward the engine car so it'll seem like it's moving when in fact it's just sitting there idle on the tracks in the yard, rusting in place for all eternity.

❖

Sleepy wet drab sad dampness in a scrubby ditch off Route 25 – but hey, least I gotta roof etc. Would rather be exposed to the cold though and climbing outta the hole my brain's dug – even falling back into it after getting a little ways up the side. But this isn't a hole I can climb out of – instead, it's like I've gotta dig my way out sideways, scooping back dirt and packing it down beneath me, gradually transforming the pit into a tomb ramp I can ascend erectly, maybe on the vernal equinox or something.

❖

I've gotta scrape enough prose together to make me a fire – string together enough words and ideas and images to keep the grammaticalothesline from seizing at the pulleys. Pulleys – I had writ *flywheels* – and then I'm reading about block & tackle and guy wires – things high up – risky things. Maybe I should climb a water tower – or one of them giant oil drums – or a derelict Little League scoreboard – or a tree in a park...

❖

A friend of mine took Astronomy 100 with me up at college. He fell asleep once in the middle of class taking notes and I always thought that piece of paper priceless. I still remember the increasingly wavery words and the way the last one just meandered across the page. Where was it he fell asleep, or what parts fell first, and how did he come back at all? We used to laugh about that page and go back to it all the time when we were studying for finals. A couple of years later he took the notebook out and we looked at it and laughed all over again. Troy. I wish I were more like Troy – always did. Not a particularly good skater or racquetballer – not an outstanding student nor the tidiest fellow – but damned if he wasn't one of the *decentest* people I've ever known. Awful funny too.

❖

Got nothing in reserve, nothing *extra* to give, no surging sense of desperation or hopelessness sufficient to kick-start any activity in my brain, spur on the dendrites, hasten a late-onset schizophrenia. I'll keep writing of course, but witness the deterioration – nay, cliff dive in quality…scope, reach, imagination. Something up there's broke – mini-stroked maybe – and *this* is what I'm left with. Why do creatures abide without incentive? Or start off living to begin with without a salient *reason* for doing so? Why did those two stupid proto-eins join together on that frothy piece of pumice? Dumb fucking luck is all – because they simply happened to be there and, as the phrase goes, 'things lined up' – billion-to-one odds prob'ly but in a universe of *this* duration billion-to-one's a bet anyone 'd take – hell, *here* even infinite odds against doesn't seem like much of a long shot…except to tenured logicians. So there isn't any luck at all really, there's just "sooner or later it's bound to happen" – most of it anyway – not happiness though – not the sort of thing *sentient beings* need – that ain't provided for in the tedium – you gotta sort that shit out yourself.

❖

New Year's Eve. So this is it for aught six. Don't give a damn – just a wall that continues out laterally as far as I can see – and me running my fingertips along it 'til I'm gone. Might submit to a grisly death if it meant a few days out of the eternal gloom shading this side – a few moments even in the empyrean splendour of the fully felt life!

But what does any of it mean, not having a chance, it seems, to get there?! It means *despair*, people – it means this place may or may not be *utterly* hopeless but that neither possibility can be ruled out – it means I've failed or am currently failing – or perhaps it don't mean nothin' at all! We keep trying, that's all we can do – *we* being the miserable and the wretched – the other fuckers don't *have* to try (and couldn't conceive what it means) – they get to set goals achievable – they are the reasonable set – banal – forget about them – *we're* the interesting ones. They get to be happy, *we* get to be interesting – fraught with interest really – punished, tortured with it.

Figure I gotta get to the bottom before I call it a year – don't have another five lines in me but that's not gonna prevent me from continuing right on down the page. Gonna pretend I'm one o' those vacuous happy fuckers and just sort of relax – chill – and talk about all the conflicts I have to invent because none exist in my life, and how I don't understand why some people seem bound and determined to be unhappy despite there being so much goodness in the world. How sad they are – how I pity them – though they have so much love in their hearts...if only they could see it. God is love people – God is love.

2007

Whatever – back to inconsequence and triviality. The carpet here is green – puce. The whole place hasn't got a single straight line. And it's in the friggin' scrub, did I mention that?! Jennie's dad sold off most of the hardwoods so the front yard – if you can call it that now – consists of stumps and the odd blighted sapling. Some of the stumps are half dug-up – some of those are charred – there is also a large pile of dirt. Yet soon – soon this dang mess 'll be a thing of the past – that is, if nothing comes along and torpedoes the deal. At this point it likely *would* take a torpedo...unless she kicks off – "Just you try...you...you ole *bitty!*" Soon we'll have our own place and our own washer/dryer and dishwasher and basement and no landlord and smack in the middle of town and maybe I'll have the job shit settled too...but you know, even if I don't, so what: our own place!

❖

Awaiting news from the job recruiter – assuming my references check out okay I'll be a working man again. How I loathe this autobiographical crap – how I long for *fictional* emprise – for scenarios in which the tedium of everyday life can be glozed, or hinted at, or ignored altogether! Who the heck wants to hear about another's daily rounds unless they're animated by something bigger: ideas – élan vital – *genius*...fleeting, mistaken, self-regarding, foolish-but-*genius* – a guiding spirit that "makes all disagreeables evaporate from their being in close relationship with Beauty and Truth."[24] Hell, it might be a ghost that "tempts you toward the flood"[25] – it might be a delusion that drives you to madness – it might be recovered faith, or a mystical genie of enlightenment, but fuck-all it's *leading* you – the damn or damnèd thing's *leading* you and all you gotta do is trust the bastard!

❖

Closing Wednesday, new job starts on Thursday – nothing else in my head – busy busy. Looking forward to moving the heck out of here – to all the changes upcoming – changes not merely for the sake of change, mind you, we're talking incontrovertibly *beneficial* changes. Of course, having settled for change would prefer it now to 've been something more radical – say, Lasik sensibility surgery – but that ain't come 'round yet, and who knows, maybe it'll be like getting Botox injections into your aesthetic gyri that wear off after a while, or silicon vocabulary implants that burst and cause fits of logorrhea.

Errands and the gym earlier – everything set for the closing. Mostly thinking about the condo though – luxuries, accoutrements – and just getting settled *into* something – life changes and whatnot – our stay in this godforsaken hovel finally reaching its merciful end. Think I may break off a piece and stick it in a vial – you know, wear it 'round my neck maybe...jab myself with it when I'm feeling blue. Wretched fucking hole, I've only been on my best behavior in case some gods showed up in disguise![26]

But perhaps we're gonna miss a few things about renting. After all, it's nice not to give a sweet damn when, say, the lintel trim falls on your head, or the faucet drip gets worse and worse, or the kitchen linoleum sags and bows, or the furnace will not work, or melt water streams down the walls and sills freezing into stalagmites on the floor, or mice and flying squirrels scurry about ceaselessly in the attic, or the tap water tastes like a bloody lip – I could go on.

❖

This guy, this regular guy, a little sadder than most perhaps, a little quieter, but otherwise fairly normal – he's out walking one day in the city and wanders off the sidewalk in a rather absent sort of way onto some old railroad tracks – you know, just taking a different route maybe – when he stumbles on a body – a homeless person it looks like. He's stunned of course, but immediately contacts the police, who later come by his apartment with a few questions. He answers them all readily enough but seems strangely distant to the interviewing officer who, when leaving, can't help but ask the guy's girlfriend, "Is he always like that?" After the police are gone his girlfriend approaches him and says, by way of reassurance, "Yes, it's strange, weird – whatever. This sort of thing happens though – like people getting hit by lightning – it happens."

Over the next couple of days he seems even quieter than usual – almost dazed. One morning a coworker asks him if anything's wrong – "No, no, I'm fine," he replies, unconvincingly. A little later he gets a call at his desk – it's a detective who'd like him to drop by the station – "at lunch – uh, o.k." When the time comes he makes his way down to police headquarters. The detective greets him at the security gate and conducts him to his office.

"So why didn't you tell us –" the detective asks, "You forget or something?"

"What?" the young man replies without energy.

"What – that's funny... – that this has happened to you before. Why didn't you tell the officer about the last time?"

"I don't know – it was a long time ago."

The detective pauses for a moment, studying the young man, then opens an old case file and pulls out an affidavit relating the discovery of a murder victim. Turns out the witness in the affidavit – the person who'd found the victim and whose identity had never been released due to his extreme youth – was this regular guy sitting there – he'd been just a boy at the time. The detective is able to get him to talk a little about the past incident, and is soon convinced that no connection could possibly exist between the two. "Seems like a pretty nice kid is all, if a bit of a loner," he thinks. Wrapping things up, he asks in an offhand manner if the young man believes in coincidences or fate, psychic powers, "You know, crap like that." No, he doesn't. And with that the detective lets him go.

A few weeks pass and the whole episode is starting to fade from the guy's mind. There's a story on the local news about a missing person – a young girl. He makes a dry comment or two but thinks little more about it. He gets up the next morning – a Saturday – and is slowly making breakfast. He's probably not going to do much that day – go back to bed maybe if his girlfriend leaves. Then the phone rings – he looks at it rather absently just before it does. It's the detective. He wants to know if the young man 'll come out and join a search party looking for that missing girl. Somehow the detective convinces him to go.

So now he's there, waiting by the roadside near some woods while things get organized, and he's met a few more cops and maybe a couple murmur something about him – he's sort of just standing off to the side – but really, they're more interested in getting their gear together. Soon he goes off with a group that's been assigned a certain section of the woods. They search walking parallel, a person every fifteen feet or so, snaking back and forth until all the ground is covered. He eats lunch with the group when the time comes – it's been provided by the girl's mother. Someone from her family asks who he is and he makes something up. Then the search resumes...and the day goes by.

At some point during the afternoon he starts to slow down a bit and fall behind. He looks off vacantly to the side, rather tired, not really thinking much at all, and catches sight of a bright colored bird or glint of something and wanders in that direction – the voices of the other searchers can still be heard. He enters a glade between some trees and sees a rock gleaming from the mica on top – must've been the rock that caught his eye – and there's moss growing on it and it looks almost like a table – a picnic rock perhaps. Picnics. He smiles a little... and then he throws up. On the other side of the rock is the missing girl.

❖

It's all inside there somewhere if only I can find the key... which probably isn't gonna happen unless I cough it up, itself a rather unlikely event.

❖

I want to set down what Grandma means to me – I want to tell you – I want to explain what it is that makes her special to me – makes losing her so terrible – catastrophic – but it all seems so stupidly obvious. It's not just her we've lost – not just her presence, her voice, her quiet tenacity for living – it's how she lived – the numinous space she sustained for us, for her husband's memory...– for me personally, it's how I felt when I came down her driveway knowing she was home – the gratitude – pride – sense of privilege even.

Sometimes while we were sitting there talking at the table I'd feel this gentle upswell of emotion and inside I'd hear myself incredulously asking, "Is she really listening to me – is she really engaged – she seems so confoundedly interested in what I have to say," and then the feeling would pass and we'd keep right on going for a long while...and then maybe I'd stack some wood.

Driving away from her house later I'd think about that feeling – about what it meant – and I never really figured it out – I think it had something to do with connecting – with trusting or understanding each other in some basic way maybe – I also think it was just me realizing how good I felt about myself when I was around her – and now that's GONE.

What would Grandma think of me up here saying these things about her? She'd be embarrassed a little I bet, but you know what she'd say? She'd say, "That was very nice, Tris." Thank you Grandma, that means a lot. I love you.

It's all gonna go away now...and I'm so exhausted from the day I can't even feel it anymore – but *this* is what happens to life – it gets sucked away one person at a time – everything and everyone we build our lives upon will eventually be stripped from us.

I don't believe in a goddamn thing except loving

despite the odds – doing it anyway, even if it's all gonna disappear. Create something that will endure – something that will deliver that love over and over and over again like a music box does a tune every time you wind it.

❖

There's nothing to be said for it – it is what it is – go to work, get out of work, come home, go to work, get out of work, come home. No life in it, no spring or pizzazz or interest, piquancy – none of it. Moved pieces of furniture around the condo last night after buying a bookcase, but they were proverbial *Titanic* deck chairs – or *Achille Lauro* anyway – not *HMS Beagle* that's fer damn sure.[27] What was I talking about anyway? – Ah, *extinction* – the origin of my specie – *change*...in my pocket. Ugh. A doubloon would be nice though. I'm not a jewelry guy but a doubloon with an outsized conquistador arrogating the motto – one of those on a nondescript gold chain – I could wear that.

❖

Same old passage of time – same old march of days – same old uncarpayed diem. Motherfucker.

Wish I felt a potentiality still – that there was still some big discovery in me yet to be made, about how to read poetry more deeply for instance, or how to see further in general, at all, at anything, askance, with welding goggles through a pin hole in a piece of paper *I don't care*, just something *more* – inches maybe – height – bigger pecs – perfect pitch – *common sense – something* I could haggle with at a street fair – at the big bazaar in my mind where everything's for sale but it's all mixed up together in unmarked bins the locals are constantly rummaging through.

Wish I had Aethra for a mom so she could just point out the secret rock under which lay all the answers.[28] And I wish I felt myself strong enough to lift it. RRRAAAAAAAHH!! – Nope, not yet – actually, not even close – I don't even think it budged.

❖

Visited the local animal shelter. Before I could choke up even a little Jennie 'd rushed back outside and burst into tears – I never had a chance. So anyway, I hate both options – not getting Reed a playmate, and having cats for life, one dying after another, always getting replaced so that the other one never gets lonely – a regular con*cat*enation – as though being a pet owner was like being the ENIAC guy running around all the time replacing those tubes.[29]

We're gonna think about it for a week I guess, then figure it out. Jennie's leaning toward, and me...I don't know – but I don't want to go through it again, ever, what happened with Abby and Keisha – losing them – and not just because I can't handle it, but also because I *had* them and they were great and so is Reed and maybe the right thing to do to honor them is not have anymore.

I walked around at lunch the other day mulling over the burning building scenario – you know, saving A versus saving B. So I thought about who I would save if I could and I put Reed on one smoky window ledge and a person on the other. I started with people I care about and kept switching them out with ones that mattered less and less 'til Fatty was pretty much getting saved without scruple (bin Laden, Dick Cheney). Anyway, I think the idea was that Reed – that *animals* – can matter to us every bit as much as people, sometimes even more, and maybe that's okay...cuz they may not know it's a terrible place with no meaning or decency, but that doesn't change the fact that it is and that we're in it together.

❖

Blustery yetch going on outside and me in here, loathsomely unbedraggled. Wish I were at a helm somewhere – i' the South Pacific, *aetat* twenty-two. Wish I was at a premiere – wish I was at a fiftieth showing! Wish I was a deckhand, a stagehand, a lent hand to any damn thing 'cept sittin' 'round here to no purpose.

Helped B. move earlier, so that was something – but the day's done for me – 's all dead until a stupid football game arrives tomorrow. I'm such a cowering toad I dare only partake of vicarity...and that but through televised sports! Don't know if I'd even read *Loves Labors Won* right now if somebody found it.[30]

I sit on the bed trying to get through a chapter or article on anything and I stop or give up or just put the book down. I feel it welling up...or trying to...but there'll need to be a lot more rain first – so much that any tears 'd be undetectable in the downpour. I look at my reflection in the mirror opposite, propped up against a wall, and I know what the likely outcomes are – that it's almost fifteen years since a *book* told me what was wrong – how unlikely it is what's hiding behind my eyes 'll ever escape – or that the warden staring back at me will ever let it out.

❖

You know what though...never mind me for a change: What about you? Tell me what *you* think – what *you* want to or ought to do – why you're reading *this* instead of tending your moon garden or jet-packing cross-continent with your friends. Are you sitting before a fire? Standing at a virtual bookstall? In Paris? Hong Kong? What's for dinner? You gotta work tomorrow? All I can do is ask questions.

❖

I hate that I have to sleep a certain way. I hate that I chew my lip. I want to live each day without effort, that's what I want – I don't want to *think* about it – I want to let *me* take over – happen – like an engine that doesn't sputter or choke, it just gohzzzzz. Isn't that the best you can do for yourself? It must be like floating along in a current and the current's in control. I got that feeling once when I was a kid on a theme park ride in Florida, twirling around in a big fat inner tube down a river lined in concrete. Come to think of it I've dreamt of that since – of riding down, with my brother behind me like on that day, or maybe alone too, or with some friends – and now it comes to mind, right when I need it: the body knows.

❖

Right there in the middle of dreaming, dead asleep, crossing a school quad or campus, with classmates all 'round, I fought against it – against vaulting into the sky – but as I walked up a berm toward the school's back entrance I thought to myself, "What *else* have I got?!", and then just *took off* – because fuck it, really, a flying dream isn't just about grandiosity – part of it's about experiencing freedom – dimensionality – power – things I lack in my waking life.

❖

Here's the difference between happy and me – happy and most. Here's all the evidence one 'd ever need to convict me of being the incorrigibly *un*happy perp in God's lineup in the sky...though what I ever did to deserve it...

So anyway, I'm at the photocopier and Happy Ted strolls on over cuz he's gotta copy something too. He greets me with what seems an energetic "How's it going today?" to which I reply, with pointed cynicism, "Couldn't be better, Ted – how 'bout you?" And then he gets kind of solemn and says, "About the same, I think." Only get this – he'd been in the bathroom like five times this morning, twice when I was in there and a couple other times besides, not that I monitor this stuff but the bathroom door closes loudly and he sits right over my cubicle wall and I can hear his chair when he sits down and...aw, never mind that! *Anyway*, point is, my goddamn life is miserable and this guy, his idea of a bad day is diarrhea (Jesus, how'd I spell that right) so fuck off, nice people! Happy Ted, good luck to you man – hope that Pepto-Bismol soothes your troubles...if that's what you're supposed to take – honestly, I'm not really even sure – when I get sick like that I just fucking *deal* with it. I'm good at that. Happy people aren't. Happy people get sick and they stupidly *feel* it. Like that makes any sense.

❖

Lest anyone – or just *me* – think I was or am a decent fellow, without supplying any excuses, let it here be recorded: No sooner had Jennie entered our domicile after bringing her mom home from the *hospital* where the latter had for several hours been undergoing a *transfusion* than I asked if she'd "had a big dinner" because of her protruding stomach. Apparently I'd also made a girth-related comment the last time she wore unsaid gray sweater, I don't remember (elephants and chicks never forget), but she became very upset. Whatever – I didn't sign up for glasses and a gut. I mean, it's not like I didn't *have* back hair before we got together. So there – that's the real me – I don't like tummies sticking out further than tits – fucking sue me.

❖

So Walter Mosley writes for like three hours every day – guess I oughtta get in here and add a little something to my bean pile. Shall I bemoan, once more, the lack of subject matter – my empty-headedness – global warming – a Patriots defeat (impossible)? Hey, how 'bout these dreams I had? In one of them some woman drowned in icy water which then froze over her – you could look right down into the ice and see the horror still imprinted on her face – oh, and psychics could commune with her. Anyway, what if, in medieval times, some queen's daughter died like that minus the creepy expression business and the gods told the queen she couldn't bury the young princess or the kingdom would fall so she spent all her wealth on erecting a temple over the place and having ice brought in to keep the pond frozen while having her chief engineer devise new mechanical ways of keeping it cold there but then she ran out of money and her starving people rebelled and she was deposed and the kingdom fell anyway...then, while the ex-queen wasted away in a dungeon, the pond melted and the people, not blaming the princess they'd all adored, gave her a beautiful and fitting funeral and buried her on a hill where she'd liked to walk and sit among the flowers. Anyhow, just a thought.

Second dream was of me with a big dog's jaws locked around my throat so this chair was rigged for me to sit in with a giant rubber band stapled to the back and the other end looped around a pole or something and they – friends qua scientists – sprang the thing with a switch and it was supposed to yank the dog off my neck but the part of the contraption that held the dog in place broke which made the chair fly back awkwardly so me and the chair and the rubber band and the safety cushions and perimeter fence all ended up in a heap and when the mess was cleared shit-all if that dog wadn't still attached to my throat! Not sure I could make a Grimm fairy tale outta that one. Walter Mosley prob'ly could.

❖

What should I have decided on way back in the winter of 19eight years old or so when I stood atop an embankment along the road up the big hill, leaning a little on my plastic sled, and pondered the slopes of life? It was more vague than that, really, but here I was, at the top of something, and I would have to come *streaking down*. I looked out over the road to the bank on the other side – I looked back behind me, down through the woods all the way to the frozen swamp at the bottom – I looked along the crest of the bank I stood on and took in all the trails I'd made so far, all the points I'd started from. Then, just like that, I swung my sled out in front of me and before it even hit the snow hurled in headfirst. That was it. I'd made up my mind. I knew how I wanted to be – what didn't matter. *What* didn't matter, Tris – get it? *What* isn't who you are – *what's* an importation – and *how* – *how* is what it is, just like frigging Yahweh... only he uses *what*. Oh, wait – he uses *that*.[31]

❖

Too many moments like this when it ain't half bad: Mummy in the shower, Fatty runnin' around yollerin' – moments that make me wonder if recording any of it ought to matter. These are the ones that get left out. Not this time.

❖

Dear Diary,

I only kept the extra roll in my closet because Jennie never ever changes the toilet paper ever and I think it's very inconsiderate to leave just a cardboard sleeve with like one tattered sheet on the dispenser all the time and expect the other person in the relationship to change it. You can't make assumptions like that, it's very selfish, and I'd rather use abrasive paper towels even than feed into her selfish lazy ways. I stand by my decision, and will do the same again if I have to. You know, maybe I'll keep that roll in my closet anyways for emergency purposes.

Dear Tris's Diary,

I think for Tris to assume I consciously do this is irrational. I, quite frankly, am just more busy than he, and in this instance did not have the time to change the aforementioned roll. This entry of his leads me to believe an incident with an empty toilet roll may have somehow scarred his memories of childhood...I will be seeking help for him – the cute little toilet paper Charmin bear will be stopping by later in the week.

Dear Diary,

It's me this time. Scarring one's memories of childhood? Surely there's some syntactical confusion there!

How do you *scar* scar tissue anyway? I mean, *really*...but what do I know. One thing's for sure, I'll never leave my damn journal open on the desktop again!

❖

This thing I saw on the internet – this picture – it just makes things so stark and hideous. Nobody's going to save us and nothing can be done to forestall chaos and annihilation – there's no extenu-melio-rating *nothing* can rationalize or excuse or explain or account for the active death of the world – the dying, all the time, the constant diminution and deterioration, the suck on all vitality. Maybe hope drains out one side and pours back in another – maybe that's what the cycle of living and death is, of evolution and extinction – maybe all life-force or imagination is recycled and nothing ever is truly lost. So fucking what?! So it's saved, it only is at the expense of others, the expense of *anything* that makes life seem worthwhile! What purpose do we serve here save to express some aspect or feature of the universe otherwise left latent? Is that this universe – what it does – just try to express everything all at once, with no regard for others...tumid and confused, a sebaceous teenage boy?! Are we all microcosmic big bangs of semiconsciousness, blasting outwards, then gradually fading away? Are we pimples bursting on his face?

2008

It's almost October now...and I'm empty – empty of human feeling, and have been for months – just 'riding it out' I guess you'd say, though the upheaval hasn't exactly been of a bracing sort, unless in the cumulative sense – *cumulatively* it's – well – Dresden circa '45 comes to mind. Really though, it's something I don't feel much like talking about – read *Darkness Visible*...or get lousy parents, if it's not too late.

I had a master plan if you can believe that – I was gonna finish the BIG WRITE, make a splash on Broadway, then get myself some serious help. Now, instead, I'm...I'm...what *am* I doing?! – I don't even know, drifting I guess, in a well-appointed very much *un*open cushy condo boat. Just drifting – haven't found a current.

Is this what the world is?! Hah – and I thought I'd prepared for the worst! I thought I could handle it...but *it* became nothing...not illness or indigence or 'beating the odds' – just nothing – hopelessness beyond despair – complete and utter nothing – plenary nothing. I was so naïve.

2009

I'm icy water circling the limbs, slowly, tortuously, deadening, dulling the urge to effort...sinking it down, then sealing up the hole!

I'm anything, really, except me – I'm a chameleon...but I only do black and white (it's a pigmentation thing).

❖

End of March...or days

Armageddon no where actually...though I haven't lost my sense of theater. Anyway, Revelations ain't happening – still stuck in Job – in working – in just getting by. Word play – that's what it is. No, it's not that either. The words don't matter – nothing at all matters – nothing sticks or holds – nothing binds or ties, not even ties, or binds. It's all shale, eroding away 'til the shelf is bare, the plateau is 0, and everything's flat again – or it was – has been since the start 'n it's only now you start to notice – but there's nothing you can do – so you write things like this, and sign off

Napoleon

❖

Wish I was filling something up like rain does – rain spilling into coursing down spouting gurgling swishing along over under...– but I've covered this before. Must be the way it doesn't care – must be its heedlessness I aspire to – envy. I envy rain – how sad is that!? I envy all things that act without forethought – all impulses that play out unimpeded, unhindered. I envy sunlight, the wind, dust, my cat, daredevils, dust devils, Lindsay Lohan, and butterflies. I do not envy moths – moths are gross.

❖

Leaked snot everywhere I went today, lubricating along like a slug. Used many tissues. Raw nose.

❖

This is it? Is this it? Is this as far as I'm gonna come? Doesn't seem even halfway up the road – the dusty summer lane that tends along the field's edge and under some trees...then over a little bridge...toward the frog pond.

❖

It's like layers of shame – like a cake with layers – or when you wear a long-sleeve shirt with a t-shirt on underneath and a coat and hat and scarf but then when you get hot you can't take anything off so you just get really sweaty and overheat. No – I guess not – it's different than that.

❖

Jennie's mom passed away. Trust me, I was there. How profane a presence – me – standing there without a thought in my head – vacant – at the foot of her bed.

2010

At work today felt a twinge when I looked outside – when outside and me caught each other's eye – and I muttered to myself, "You know what you're doing? It's like you're hiding behind a chair." And it probably is. I can recognize that – but you know, big deal – *outside* recognized it for fuck sake.

❖

It's like emptiness swallowed by nothing then voided. Like a featureless timeline, calipers slipping off at the ends. Like a journey across Antarctica with unremitting cold and snow and ice. Like a thing not worth supplying a simile.

❖

Thought today, during the one moment not subsumed by my stupid job, that I oughtta try to write about something...*anything*, other than self – try to keep from diary entries 'n dry daily reports – from discussing writing and future and past and family and friends and cat – from dismay and ennui and malaise and indifference. What would I be writing about, then? Or would I be a disembodied spirit floating around and through shit incapable of mortal sense? But I don't want to inhabit space anymore – what I want is to people *mind* – to multiply self – to split off and regrow and send out suckers and evolve away from the Einsteinian *here*.

Last week I went to the library for the first time in months. I get off on the fourth floor like I always do and just start walking the aisles, scanning the shelves 'til I pull something down and go find a place to sit – it's a centenary book of Melville criticism. And I read an essay about his time in the Custom House and how that fits his bio – as though anything fits any other goddamn thing – you think that train wreck *fits* Dickens?! So anyway, I walk outta there thinking yeah, I'm maybe putting in some time at the Custom House – better now than later, I suppose... though a Patent Office might be preferable.

My method is so fucking agreeable – so exasperatingly reassuring – the way I wrap the thing 'round and cinch it with a fibula – the way I have to tie it all up – Einstein and the Patent Office. Always so desperate to plug the leaking rhetoric – to cap the spill. I wish I could allow that everything's wide open – that I could relax and let it *be so* – because then I wouldn't try to ring the slick with boom and burn it off – I'd just let it float, pollute the shore, upset the equilibrium. Who knows, maybe then it wouldn't even be oil anymore – or not the big toxic mess I always envision.

Tidy little bows topping every piece of me. Howz about ribbon instead of bows?! Open-ended instead of closed – Möbius fucking ribbon – MFR – kinda like OSB, only not as practical.[32]

❖

Did you know there's not a single article or story online about Secretariat's personality? All the wonderful race footage and testimonials to his beauty and strength and perfect conformation, but the most I could find about *him* was that he'd run up to visitors at his paddock, then gallop off at full speed and charge back again. "A magnificent animal," I've read again and again. It's the race callers that seem to express true esteem, that assess his awesome performances – at least in part – as a measure of *character*. For most everyone else it's about endurance and drive and strength and breeding – imagination never enters into it. But when Chic Anderson says Secretariat is "moving like a tremendous machine" he's not talking about an animal at all, he's talking about a person – he's talking about you and me – he's saying that this horse has personality, an intelligence and spirit and self-awareness that set him apart. And he does. He absolutely does.

❖

Just to say I did I've opened this thing and commenced typing thoughts, or thought process, or traces of neuronal activity, or...whatever's even less connected with THE AFFAIRS OF THE WORLD. Because, well, you know: I'm not connected with them – not to politics or human rights or the FBI – none of it. Now, I *do* have a vested interest in the local weather system, as well as the condition of my elbows and knees. I've got capital tied up right now in...in there being a tennis court available one hour from now at the local high school. But it's a narrow, parochial interest, is it not? – I mean, provided I can play, do I really care what happens to the Wilkins ice shelf in the meantime? I do not.

Let's try this one more time. Okay...so I just sat down to make a record of the movements in my mind – and if by *significant* are denoted those movements planetary or interstellar, well then, the kind I'm talking about are more to marble scale – to beat-up little aggies skittering across a sandy parking lot toward some near inaudible impact. But even so, the impact does make a sound – at least I'm not trying to use my brain in outer space or when a tree falls in the woods and no one else is around. And at least here it may be possible to make a difference with the thing, if only I can get it to work right...like a stubborn magic eight ball you keep shaking and jiggling and gingerly tapping 'til finally it flattens a polyhedronal face against the scratched plastic pane for all to see: *Reply hazy, try again.*

❖

Happy people. They sometimes remind me of a physicist's 'flatlanders,' the two-dimensional inhabitants to whom fourth-dimensional travelers might compare us earthlings. Not to have any tragic depths – to be a flatlander – from the point of view of a *damaged person* like myself: how very idyllic...and how very boring. If the world were replete with 'em there'd be no wars or terror, but there'd be precious little progress either. Here occurs to me a somewhat radical and not altogether tongue-in-cheek conception – that they're a different psychological species. Yeah, we can mate with 'em and make donkeys or ligers or whatever, but there's a fundamental difference in the psychological mechanisms of us and them – bit of a Morlock and Eloi kinda thing only without the eating – or maybe those in Limbo versus the Saved.[33]

❖

Raining hard – possible "tornadic activity" at some point if the TV's to be trusted. No tennis or walk or interest or empathy for anybody or anything: Depression, year the third. Is it that long since I wrote something of moment, thought something of value? All those days, just gone, many surrendered without a fight at all – and *this* – is this me fighting – these monomonotonous plaints – these repedundant ruings?! Honestly, what writing, what subject matter, is gonna make any difference at this point? Just go back and look – no, don't waste your time, but take my word for it, I've tried to touch on it all – I've tried to take in my hands every slippery eel from every slimy crevice of my brain, tried to hold each oleaginous one for just long enough...'til they'd squirt away and dart back down to their caves.

Getting some thunder now. Winds picking up. This is what I need. Like a conjurer, seeking the elements in commotion...

Where was I?

Precisely: lost.

Sheesh, it's getting really dark.

❖

But if I could see the world from a new vantage – see *into* it from *out*side – if I could stick my arms into a wormhole coat – thrust 'em into *the sleeves of time!* Well, yes – if I could – but I cannot.

❖

Been picking berries lately – cherries on Thursday out back, blackberries yesterday evening at Jennie's Dad's. For me, berry picking is meditative. I can relax yet I don't have to contort myself into funny poses or live under a tree at the top of a mountain. There is some stooping involved though. And some berry picking is actually done at the top of mountains, but it isn't mandatory picking, and you don't have to stay there through bad weather or meet the expectations of pilgrims who've trudged up for enlightenment. You can eat the fruits of your meditation too, always a nice perk, and one which surely beats trying to figure out the sound of a single berry clapping. And you can bring the berries home to sprinkle on your oatmeal or bake into muffins or pies. And you don't have to protect the berries from a rival sect, employing monkish kung-fu. Berries sometimes smear on your hands a little so that can be a drag – but better that than sit on your pinkies for hours on end not talking to anyone.

    We've got highbush blueberries right here in Portland growing out in people's yards. Even now raspberries are ripening at the edge of the parking lot outside this window! And I'd recommend a trip to Maxwell's in Cape Elizabeth to anyone who visits Maine this time of year. Sure, take in the lighthouses and the sea air, but then stop by there to pick strawberries and eat them in the heat. It's my belief that optimal strawberry gustation can only be achieved at temperatures over 80°, and even then, only while standing in a field surrounded by other pickers intent on the same. In fact, I guarantee a taste test would prove that strawberries are better in company. I can't explain exactly why, but I think there's something cheerful and engaging in the taste that encourages sociability. The blueberry is a different animal – more solitary – maybe because it's dusky blue instead of jolly red – or maybe because of something spritely in the flavor – something of the woodland nymph, of a bygone era – something wistful – even sorrowful – blue. Blackberries are hardy and muscular creatures; they don't rot as much as their raspy brethren; they glisten more and hold their form; they come in more generous bunches and, if you'll only brave the prickers, the picking can be bountiful. Sure, the taste lacks some of the subtlety and undertones – the symphonic *notes* – of the Great Berries – but, for relative ease of picking and a generous if uncomplicated taste quotient, it makes a good starter berry, just as the recorder makes a good starter instrument for children. The cherry is...well, I don't really want to go too far into it but it grows on a damn tree – you reach up instead of out or down, and that's just not berry picking to me, it's more like browsing – and I can forget about the pits but the skin – the skin just does not live up to the Great Berries.

If you know about the Great Apes than you'll understand what I mean by the "Great Berries" – orangutans, chimps, gorillas – blueberries, raspberries, strawberries – it's that simple – and there are doubtless direct correlations between members of both groups. For instance, don't orangutans and raspberries line up nicely, or blueberries and bo-...– wait a minute – I just remembered: *bonobos*. I forgot all about bonobos. So there are four Great Apes – four – and only three Great Berries. Shit-all if that doesn't throw a, uh, certain kind of *wrench* into the proceedings. And USA is down 1-nil against Ghana – fucking Ghana. That's probably where bonobos come from.

❖

Last night at a wedding rehearsal dinner I accidentally banged our table pretty hard and my dad disowned me...or, I mean, he *would have* if he'd ever bethought himself of owning to begin with. Sure he pays for things and doesn't mind letting on to the fact with needling reminders like, say, laughing demonstratively from a prominent seat at a wedding rehearsal dinner in the middle of several toast speeches, or, just generally, *reminding* – but owning like taking care of, responsibility for, caring about – well...not so much. But hey, lest we forget, it was me upset the table, proper and metonymic; it was me who got carried away with my Robert Goulet stylings; me who booed while others clapped at the middle school love letter sentiments recited by one of the bride's sisters; and yes, again, it was me who obstreperously struck our damn table with more force than intended...and now I'm paying the price, which is not the same as when my dad pays – I'm just a little ashamed is all, he's the one out like ten thousand bucks.

Now, things got trickier when Jennie started crying because she'd tried to settle my dad down and he didn't *pay* any attention to her – dicier still when, at Jennie's behest cuz she couldn't stop crying, I walked her to the lady's room and, while waiting outside, my sister confronted and flayed me – or when, having risen from the table to make said retreat, my stepmother remarked, albeit tentatively, "Well, I guess we'll see you tomorrow then," to which I quickly retorted, "We're not *leaving* – we'll be back in a few minutes." Then come to find out it was almost a year ago today that Jennie's mom took her mortal digger (sorry Joyce, but it didn't have to be this way if you'd just *taken a walk once in a while*).

Well anyway, somewhere in there it was that I realized, egg dribbling down my nose: I'd blundered into the perfect confection. Yes, suddenly there it was, like an apparition before me, ingredients already measured and poured, spatula verily spiriting itself around in the mixing bowl...and a culinary familiar, hovering nearby, licking a glutinous finger.

❖

Boom! Pow! Damn the torpedoes! Ramming speed! Mayday Mayday!! A call to action or sound mayhap thereof – a summons to some war council or capital t Tribunal – an awakening of – reinvigoration – *renaissance*! Just to purpose again instead of blunder[buss]ing about – to set down something which seemeth marble – alabaster – jade. Something chiseled, incised – something with permanence – not "Croatoan" carved in a tree.[34] Do you understand what I mean?

❖

The people were all talking – you know, saying people stuff, being secretive and cagey-like – same old chestnutty wont – befuddling themselves with all that lying and hiding and covering up. There they were, doing that again, and me trying not to, in the opposite corner... as it were...with mixed success.

2011

I got nothing – nothing the least revealing – nothing that helps allays assuages any of the hollow emptiness of naught – or knot – can a knot be hollow? Then I'm a hollow knot on a tree. I'm a burl. I'm a dead branch. I'm kindling. I'm flame in a fire. I'm burning. But I'm cold too, like ice. I'm frost. I'm that Frost poem about fire and ice. No, I'm shellfish. Yes, shellfish, and I'm allergic to myself – my face gets all puffy and I can't breathe when I eat one of my appendages. So I'm a shellfish that's allergic to itself but also, I've got tiger blood.

All this word association reminds me: I like the taste of envelope glue. Or rather: I don't *mind* the taste of envelope glue. The guy who sits next to me at work is always trying to convince me that I should use a gluestick to seal letters instead of my tongue. So I say to him, because he likes bacon, "I bet if the envelopes tasted like bacon, you'd use your tongue too," and he shoots back, "I'm gonna look that up!" Five minutes later he's found this website called *Mmmvelopes.com* and sure as shit that's what they sell, envelopes with bacon flavored glue. So I ask him to look up envelope flavored bacon. He says that's stupid.

Somehow or other I don't feel like that anecdote quite reached the "penetralium of the mystery."[35] A soliloquy might do it...if I could manage one...but I can't. I could assay a line or two and then give up...? Whaddya think? Yeah, sure, give it a try:

Is it thus the end comes?
Or is there some more meaningless elision –
Elipses – no keyboard can account for?
It must be so.

Didn't Kean die in the middle of *Othello*?[36] And there was that Polonius who fell off a ladder and broke his neck during a show. Of course, that's not the usual. Most of us collapse in the wings – that's just how it is. Also, most of us are extras.

❖

There's little life beyond the mundane, the everyday, the dirty half melt former snow, the scabby branch-broken saplings Public Works crews over-zealously planted in late October, the potholed streets and plow-shorn sidewalk strips of grass, and Christmas trash, and dog waste spring thaws reveal like icemen in the Alps, or mastodon tasted by a czar – wretched Romanov – Kirilov – Rachmaninoff... – serge. What the heck is that anyway?

❖

A pen in the hand is worth two in the uh...jar being used to hold pens. I very nearly erased that but, tired and drained though I well may be, I'm gonna fight through it to come up with an entry – I did not say insight – *entry*. Here goes: ...nothing. Hold on – wait – let me try again. And...nope. How 'bout if I punch myself in the arm? Pluck out a hair from my head? Count retreating sheep as they climb backwards over the fence hind legs first? Make another cup of brew on the stupid new coffeemaker I didn't need in the first place but Jennie's dad gave it to me so I kept it and sent the old one down the basement stairs into languishment with the holiday decorations, expired cans of soup and, oh yeah, that plastic bin full of my writing. I could continue with an inventory of all the crap we have stored down there but I won't because it's just stuff cluttering up an insignificant corner of the world...and because a lot of it is Jennie's shoes.

❖

Another one uh them damn tsunamis but I'm not gonna write about it except to say, "Sendai," much as I may or may not have uttered "Banda Aceh" a few years back. The merest signposts here, sad to say, though I can feel the surge sweep past, the cars and mailboxes, sofas and ragged corpses bobbing about in mock merriment. Watched a few brief clips on YouTube and under one a guy commented, ":13 the nearest white car has a person in it." Reminds me of a 9/11 clip I watched that synched up a shot of the South Tower just before it went down with this poor bastard's cell phone call – he says something about looking out broken windows and maybe what floor he's on and then...there's the scream. But I'm like that sign – or the hollow steel tube it clung to, tilted sideways a little after colliding with a truck – an upside down half-submerged pickup truck – and man, I wish I could be that truck, the way it can't see where it's going or have an inkling even what'll happen to it. Wish I could plunge through a city center then float out to sea like that truck – I would certainly trade being a signpost for being that truck.

❖

Not really thinking of anything much at all, but thinking-I-should-think, *that's* got me thinking. It's puzzlement more than excitement – confusion more than expectancy. Mind over doesn't matter.

Huh, I wonder if that's what drives me to write, an instinctive sense, not of the jumble and chaos which makes up our perceived world, but of the *underneath* as just a smooth sphere, featureless and devoid, to which meaning scarcely clings. Maybe writing is just a trying on of meanings, like in a dressing room maybe, or on a mannequin. Maybe that Styrofoam-filled plastic torso – maybe every writer has one – and they punk it out, make it hip or fey or tween it – just see what fits – what style, I mean. Mine is one of those super chic ebon models, über thin with three thatches of perfectly contoured hair. Ooh la la!

❖

Went over my bro's house to check on his cats – he's away on vacation. Man, he uses a lot more kitty litter than me! His litter boxes were like sandboxes, or maybe small dykes – and there were these little turds buried way underneath that seemed like they'd shriveled up – desiccated – I mean, these were borderline coprolites. But I guess that sort of thing happens when the litter's like six inches deep. Which reminds me – I still haven't seen that "2 girls 1 cup" video. I've watched "Drama Squirrel" like fifty times but I haven't yet made time for the shit-eaters. Gotta work that into my schedule somehow.

❖

It hurts all the more to write this stuff after watching a play. Just back from B.'s bean supper & radio plays – they weren't particularly memorable – still, listening to the words being read from the scripts was a painful experience. I drove off after the briefest of goodbyes to B.'s parents and girlfriend, not because I actually thought I was rushing home to write, but the pretense of urgency – the fantasy – made those few minutes zipping through red lights and traffic seem purposeful...and that seeming's about as close to real as I get. Mostly I feel a purpose about on par with one of those plastic dividers at the supermarket. So...here's my question: Am I Miltonically marking time or merely serving to separate people's grocery items?[37]

❖

Good Friday, attempt the first:

A flimsy plastic cake topper shaped like a cross
Sits squarely centered in our window –
As I wash my hands in the kitchen sink
I noticed that it's bleeding. Cue angelic chorus!
Wait, never mind, that isn't blood –
Unstuck from the glass it leaves a greasy smear –
Jesus wouldn't do that. Nope.
Jennie didn't clean the icing off the back.

Second effort:

There, centered in our kitchen window, *J'accusing*,[38]
A plastic cross pealed off a Walmart cake,
Stuck there to make us think of Easter,
And all the nice things we have that,
Without our dear Lord's sacrifice,
Might belong to someone else.

Giving up:

Fucking ay Jesus I'm trying to write a poem about you and you just won't let me. Guide my goddamn hand you...you stubborn Jew! Or if you can't do that, at least bless my Keno card before I drop it off tomorrow when I get to Foxwoods, because I'd really like to win some money so I can celebrate my love for you in a quiet beachside retreat. I'm thinking Fiji but I'm sure we could work something out.

❖

Indeed it must be that I don't at heart wish to be a writer, for in selecting from my CD collection a playlist meant to inspire, I find I've chosen an unfinished symphony and an incomplete mass!
R. has mentioned it, or we've touched on the subject anyway – more than once – that perhaps I chose writing rather out of a need to achieve than as that vocation to which I might otherwise have been most naturally drawn. Well, if that's the case, then I have no vocation – nothing pleases me to do. Bah! It's writing...or retribution and suicide – and so far, with so little good accomplished, methinks I'm well along the retributive path toward that bridge whence I hurl me.
Been thinking a lot lately about how shallow I've become – or at least that the deep end of the pool needs dredging...though they don't do that with pools. Anyway, you can get your prostate scraped but your brain...it ends up like a clogged trap...a silted up seed bed. I feel like there's all these chasms and trenches I still could reach if I had a submarine or an ROV, but why do I need them – why – when emerging all around me are skin divers with *giant pearls*?!

Hit the reset button – shake the Etch A Sketch – fire the drill. Trying not to pick up where I left off – trying to figure out some other approach, hatch another strategy – but I can't – there's nothing – ingenuity...and emptiness underneath – empty space rather – a chasm indeed.

Schubert wrote 600 lieder...and some ciphery schlub out there's prob'ly penned three thousand washing machine manuals! But no one yet disturbs the tomb of Qin Shi Huang.

❖

Found a wood piece in my box of raisins. It was bound to happen I suppose. I mean, the warning's right there on the side of the box. Still, I never thought it'd happen to *me*. Like getting busted for illegal downloads or kidnapped by aliens or something: that shit happens to *other* people. This one time a fungus was growing on a corn pop in my cereal – looked like a little orange sea anemone – but it didn't strike me as surreal. Not like the wood piece. That wood piece made me think about *mortality* – about what a meaningless fuckin' ride it all is if I end up blue on the floor, choked out by yeah, you guessed it, a tiny piece of wood. My mom called Poison Control once after I ate some mushrooms in the backyard and I remember, years later, taking down that bottle of Ipecac from behind the mirror...you know, just to feel the heft of it, like maybe it was an old sling stone I was gonna use on destiny again. We had a mutual respect, me and that black plastic out of date decoction – there was "comity" between us, same as Cokie Roberts claims Betty Ford would've urged in this debt ceiling debate. But not so with the wood piece – it had other, darker designs. All of which calls to mind *poems*, one by yours truly and one by Pound. Here they are, in no particular order:

> I make a pact with you, Walt Whitman –
> I have detested you long enough.
> I come to you as a grown child
> Who has had a pig-headed father;
> I am old enough now to make friends.
> It was you who broke the new *wood*,
> Now is a time for carving.
> We have one sap and one root –
> Let there *be commerce between us.*

~

> A dove flew down on a ray of light
> It landed on my hand and shite.
> I beat that bird with all my might
> But it stayed white and quite upright,
> Unmoved by either slight or smite,
> So instead I tried to be polite –
> *Me and that* magic angel bird,
> We talked a while then laughed all night.

(Italics are mine – I've always wanted to say that!)

And there you have it – a typical entry – can't seem to manage more than that – than falling back on the voice of levity, persona of non grata – poseur-ism. Really, I know these squibs get me nowhere, yet somehow I still feel the wind through my hair...or, that is, through the filamental projections of my digital self.[39]

Today's work koan: "Why do I not wake up each morning thrilled to be alive?" And I meditated and cogitated and phlegmatically expectorated this all day... and you know what I came up with? Squat. Nothing. Nihil. Nada. Am I not grateful to be here – grateful as many a man that's dead? I imagined Cummings – not ee but Bruce – playfully poking me in the ribs, saying, "Hey old man, I'll finish that life there if you're not going to," like it was a half-eaten bag of fries. Keats too would be right there to finish 'em up, ketchup-filled ramekins at the ready. Catullus though, he'd likely season 'em with some exotic spice, not to mention he'd call 'em Gaul fries... or that the Romans didn't have potatoes. Schubert, portly fellow, you know he'd dig right in – hell, he'd eat McNuggets off the floor – sorry Franz, but you know it's true. Raphael, he – well – he doesn't seem like a fried food kind of guy – in fact, I don't think caffeinated soda'd be a good idea for him. Caravaggio – he wouldn't even friggin' ask, and you *know* he'd wipe his mouth on his sleeve. Marlowe, Mozart, Masaccio – I could go on. It's like I keep all the ones that died young in a different part of my brain than the rest, with a frialator. It isn't fair – no, not that they died young, though *that* surely isn't either – no, what's not fair is that I torment myself with their examples – that I make mantras of Marlowe, Mozart, Masaccio, because they lived historic-ly...in such short spans.

❧

Still, same as ever, I feel it nagging and gnawing, the mystery of what I'm meant to do. And I don't mean *meant* as in some perfect purpose or keystone in a grand design. That's just hooey. I mean something more modest, stripped down, more nakedly honest – I mean the craft or avocation or happenstance endeavor that'll make the nag and gnaw *go away*. And I'm not talking fitful reprieves either. No – peace of mind, doggonit! "Serenity now!"[40] It seems foolish to ask, but can you get that here? Is it available, like side airbags or jimmies – like selling yer soul to make a buck – or everything else to join the Peace Corp? People can do those things – they can hoard all their karmic capital then go on a spending spree – but they can't buy happiness. I hate how inescapably trite that is – how trite and true. How populist. How down to earth. How close to the soil and odor of decay. And Lee Greenwood songs.

❖

Nothing worth preserving – not from the off days between starts, as a pitcher might say. Too many off days. Too much side work and throwing in the bullpen when I wanna be *in the game*. I don't care if ten guys in a row hit homeruns off me. Fans could be heckling from the stands saying it looks like I'm throwing BP. I could be out there pitching in my underwear – an old pair – but I'd hardly notice if I was *in the game*. Last week and a half I've had no fire at all and it makes me feel worthless, stupid and worthless – like I'm just taking up space on the roster. Goddamnit. God fucking god damn damnit is all I have to say. How long canna fella rub up a ball? How many sunflower seeds can he chew? Damnit. Damnit. Damnit. Come back to me oh muse, I don't give a shit about baseball – that was just a metaphor. Alack.

❖

Looked at all the websites, contemplated all the dreams, and once again gave up looking without having filed a single application. Couple of postings that caught my eye: aircraft de-icer and ticket agent for a regional airline. Don't know but that the romance of travel gets me when I see that stuff, and truth be told, I do like to linger in airports – the bigger the better. I like to leave Jennie at our gate and walk as far as Customs and Passport Control will permit. I do the same, to an extent, at Port Authority – I even try at South Station. Yes, the romance and allure – the thought that people are moving purposefully – that, surely, if they've gone to the trouble to get themselves to an airport, it's because they've got somewhere to go. And since I don't, existentially speaking... you know...*have* anywhere to go, even when I am indeed going, it's liberating to just join the flow of sprightly humanity as it courses through the corridors, pulsates through the halls. For a time the IV Drip of Despair trails behind me, though the tube still ruefully tugs at my arm.

❖

Jennie's trying on clothes again after losing, as she puts it, "a bunch of weight" – as if she'd gathered it up and tied it off in a sack. Good for her. Anyway, she left one of the sliding doors to her closet open again and you should see inside there, it's like a giant compost heap of clothing. I bet if I dug to the bottom there'd be a pulpy mass of dyes and thread – and I swear the thing gives off heat! Wait, that was fun, I'm gonna try it again: Jennie's closet is like a rainforest with its network of viney straps dangling from the canopy and all manner of odoriferous ecosystems, some redolent of blossoming orchids, others emitting swamp gas, just as the mushroomy Renuzit's chanced to be placed, or the irregular freshets of extra strength Febreze do or do not penetrate the damp.

Shall I offer my own closet in contrast? Um, no... perhaps not – that might expose *me* to a criticism or two. Hey, so I'm neat – big deal. So the coat hanger colors tend to match the shirts – I said *tend*. Fact is, there's a pile of clothes in my closet just as in hers, but it's managed see, that's the difference – it's under control – by which I mean it's in a hamper, consists entirely of dirty clothes, and shows up blue on infrared scanners.

❖

If Gronkowski played for Denver I think I'd have to move – topical enough for you? Think I'll let it just sit there at the top of this entry. Not that I have substantially more to say. Not that any further insight's happened upon me since last night when I lay in bed refreshing CBS Game Tracker on Jennie's phone. It hung for the longest time on a minute eight – turns out some crazy guy had run onto the field. Jennie had her head propped up on an elbow, dozing in and out of attention. I was riveted. Because I felt sure I knew what was going to happen. And lo, it did.

All of us want to believe in something greater than ourselves, a higher purpose or benevolent design in human affairs (*in rebus hominum*). Sometimes that want becomes aligned with an event or a series or sequence of events or happenings. And sometimes, rarely, under a unique set of circumstances to be sure, it seems to manifest itself in and through the actions of a single man. Ladies and gentleman, *Ecce* that man.

And now, let us lower ourselves upon one collective knee and pray: Almighty God, creator of football and heaven, allow Tim Tebow to keep doing this crazy stuff as long as he's able because it's really, really exciting and feeds the hope that everything we ever thought about the quarterback position – and by extension about life – can be routed out and turned on its ear! Amen.

Worms Don't Have Appendices

Dear Mr. or Ms. Agent,

I know that our publishing houses consider it virtually impossible for a true literary work, even one of the highest distinction, to achieve a commercial success on the order of, say, a *Harry Potter* installment, or an unauthorized celebrity bio. Nor do I expect market strategists from the leading houses to know just what to do with a hybrid work that purports to be equal parts nonfiction, memoir, poetry, and spiritualism. But do something they must because my book, *The Annelid Poet*, will craven even the most entrenched skeptics!

Presented in the form of an occasional journal, *The Annelid Poet* swings from meditation to vituperation, vernacular to blank verse, and tenderness to wrath, all in the space of a single page – a voice withal so versatile as must marvel the reader with its capaciousness. Can so many moods and tones be yet one man? Behold the Annelid! (And uh...expect to apply for a trademark on this name.)

The Annelid does not discuss current events, or politics, or conspiracy theories, nor does he insist upon any particular opinions really except to suggest or imply or cry out: *I do not understand!* He is a playboy (in spirit), a philosopher par excellence, and a penetrating critic – he is also extremely sensitive. A blurb on the dust jacket of this epic hundred forty page tome might proclaim, with a certain stock seriousness: "By turns forthright, intimate, funny, morose, poetic, manly, and mystical, this always engaging book charts one writer's ongoing, passionate search for meaning in a world full of contraries, antinomies, and doubt." On the other hand, this is just such a book as might benefit the more from one of those quotes by a misguided poet lariat or laureate or whatever who says, "*The Annelid Poet* is a mess. I don't know what this guy was thinking."

The market for such a robust tour de force of nonfiction, memoir, and poetry, will be broad enough to include readers with any one of these interests. And, whereas *The Annelid Poet* is written by a young man in something of a protracted spiritual crisis, you may count upon the wholehearted support of Generation X-ers.

No, he did not intend to set the literary firmament afire, but the Annelid has fashioned something quite startlingly original: an eminently readable diary of a literary artist, replete with poetic accounts and prose reflections *of the highest distinction*.

May I send you a copy of the completed manuscript? I look forward to hearing from you soon. Thank you for your time and patience.

Respectfully,

The Annelid

Notes

[1] Rocinante was Don Quixote's broken-down old hack; Bucephalus, the mighty warhorse of Alexander the Great.
[2] Robert Frost, "The Wood-Pile"
[3] *Macbeth* III.iii.109-111
[4] John Keats, "On Seeing the Elgin Marbles"
[5] Cf. *Macbeth* V.v.20
[6] Keats, "This Living Hand Now Warm and Capable"
[7] Translation: "Yet what is this?" Friedrich Hölderlin, "Mnemosyne," third version. I don't know a lick of German but there's something desperate in the line. For me it encapsulates the anguished incomprehension that Hölderlin, struggling unsuccessfully against mental illness at the time of this revision, must have felt toward the common reality...which was slowly retreating from view.
[8] Daphne was the chaste daughter of the river god Peneus. The Olympian god Apollo became enamored of Daphne and, when she fled from him, chased after her. The pursuit brought them near the river and, just as Apollo was on the verge of catching her, Daphne called upon her father to protect and save her from the amorous god. In response to her supplications Peneus transformed Daphne into a laurel tree, which Apollo ever after held sacred.
[9] *C.H.U.D.*, dir. Douglas Cheek, C.H.U.D. Productions & New World Pictures, 1984
[10] Cf. Keats, "Welcome Joy, and Welcome Sorrow"
[11] Franz Schubert, Op. 26 (D. 797)
[12] See the first three lines of "The Second Coming," by William Butler Yeats
[13] Reference to the stairs in the vestibule of the Laurentian Library at Florence, designed by Michelangelo
[14] Frost, "After Apple-Picking"
[15] Captain James Cook (1728-1729), notable British explorer, navigator, and cartographer
[16] Keats, "Lines on Seeing a Lock of Milton's Hair"
[17] Keats, letter to George & Georgiana Keats (February 14 – May 3, 1819)
[18] Keats, "On First Looking into Chapman's Homer"
[19] Cf. Pink Floyd, lyrics from "Time" and "Breathe," *The Dark Side of the Moon*, Harvest Records & Capitol Records, 1973
[20] Cliff-face formation once found in the White Mountains of New Hampshire, it collapsed in 2003

[21] Cf. William Shakespeare, sonnet 129
[22] Reference to the thought experiment devised by Austrian physicist Erwin Schrödinger (1887-1961) to illustrate an unusual feature of quantum mechanics
[23] Percy Bysshe Shelley, "Hymn to Intellectual Beauty"
[24] Keats, letter to George & Tom Keats (December 21, 1817)
[25] *Hamlet* I.iv usually around line 70, depending on the edition
[26] Allusion to the mythical tale of Baucis & Philemon, found in Ovid's *Metamorphosis*, book VIII. Baucis & Philemon are an elderly couple of very limited means visited by two strangers ostensibly in need of food and shelter. All of their neighbors have turned the strangers away but Baucis & Philemon welcome them into their modest home, laying out their best tablecloth and serving what coarse food they have with great hospitality. When the strangers are revealed to be the gods Zeus and Hermes the humble couple falls to praying for the gods' indulgence. The gods transform the house of Baucis & Philemon into a temple and appoint the two its lifelong guardians...right after flooding the rest of the village in punishment for the ill treatment they'd received from everyone else.
[27] The *Achille Lauro* was a mid-sized cruise liner with a calamitous history that included fires, a collision with another vessel, and a hijacking by terrorists; *HMS Beagle* was the ship on which naturalist Charles Darwin visited South America and the Galapagos Islands as part of a British scientific expedition.
[28] Aethra was the mother of Theseus, a semi-mythical Greek hero. King Aegeus (the Aegean Sea is named for him, but that's another story) was his father. Before unconscionably abandoning poor Aethra and son in the tiny backwater of Troezen, Aegeus hid a pair of his sandals and a sword under a huge boulder there. The king instructed Aethra that, if ever the boy grew strong enough to lift the boulder, he should seize these tokens of his parentage and journey to Athens to claim his birthright...which, in due course, he did.
[29] The ENIAC was an important early computer that used vacuum tubes as relay switches. It was an enormous machine and the tubes, which became quite hot during operation, had a very high failure rate.
[30] *Loves Labors Won* is a lost play by Shakespeare
[31] Exodus 3:14 "And God said unto Moses, I AM THAT I AM" (King James version)
[32] For "Möbius ribbon," cf. Möbius strip. OSB is an acronym for oriented strand board, a versatile building material.

[33] The Morlock and the Eloi are two races of primitive humanoids in H.G. Wells's novel, *The Time Machine*. The groups live somewhat in balance, with the subterranean Morlocks – who come out only at night – treating the docile and otherwise helpless Eloi rather like cattle, and relying upon them as a primary food source.

[34] "Unexplained letters found (1590) carved on a tree on Roanoke Island off North Carolina by Governor John White when he returned to the colony from England and discovered the colonists gone. White took the letters to mean that the settlers had moved to Croatoan Island some fifty miles away, but no trace of them was ever found." *The Columbia Electronic Encyclopedia*, 6th ed. 2007, Columbia University Press

[35] Keats, letter to George & Tom Keats (December 21, 1817)

[36] Edmund Kean (1789-1833), eccentric English actor perhaps best known for his Shakespearean roles

[37] See the sestet of John Milton's sonnet, "On His Blindness"

[38] From *J'accuse*, the name of an open letter published in 1898 by the French writer & activist Emile Zola (1840-1902), charging the French government with anti-Semitism and unlawful imprisonment in the case of army officer Alfred Dreyfus, who had been convicted of espionage and sentenced to penal servitude for life at the notorious Devil's Island.

[39] Line adapted from *The Matrix*, dir. Andy & Lana (formerly Larry) Wachowski, Warner Bros, 1999

[40] *Seinfeld*, episode 159, NBC, airdate October 9, 1997

Made in the USA
Middletown, DE
04 May 2018